The Jewel in the Lotus

The Jewel in the Lotus
A Guide to the Buddhist Traditions of Tibet

Edited and with an Introduction by
Stephen Batchelor

Wisdom Publications London

First published in 1987

Wisdom Publications
23 Dering Street
London W1, England

British Cataloguing in Publication Data
The Jewel in the lotus: a guide to the
    Buddhist traditions of Tibet.
    1. Buddhism—China—Tibet
    I. Batchelor, Stephen
    294.3'923   BQ7604

ISBN 0 86171 048 7

Set in Bembo 11 on 13 point by Characters of Taunton, Somerset and printed and bound by Eurasia Press of Singapore on 80gsm cream Sunningdale Opaque paper supplied by Link Publishing Papers of West Byfleet, Surrey.

Contents

Preface

Many books have been published in recent years on Tibetan Buddhism, yet almost all draw upon the teachings of only one of the four major traditions alive today – Nyingma, Kagyu, Sakya and Geluk. This certainly points to the richness and vastness of the Tibetan tradition, for each of the four schools has been found to possess a wealth of oral and written teachings, much of which still remains unknown to the rest of the world. While this task of deepening our understanding of the particular traditions continues, a need exists for a book to introduce newcomers to all four.

For this present anthology I have selected short, representative texts composed by major teachers from each school and have arranged them in chronological order. Hopefully, this will enable the reader to appreciate the range of teachings given in Tibetan Buddhism and will provide an authoritative overview of the religion. We must bear in mind, however, that these writings reveal only a tiny fraction of the entire corpus of Tibetan spiritual literature. They have been chosen on account of their pragmatic and experiential qualities. In addition to these more accessible teachings, Tibetan canonical and extra-canonical works cover a wide range of texts dealing with subjects as diverse as logic, philosophy, psychology, cosmology, tantric ritual, medicine and poetry.

In the introduction to the anthology itself I have tried to outline the historical context in which Tibetan Buddhism emerged and to give an account of the central views and beliefs held in common by all Tibetan Buddhists. Although I have sought to be as objective and impartial as possible, I recognize that much of what I say will inevitably reflect my own training as a monk in the Geluk tradition.

This introduction first appeared in a serialized form under the title *The Jewel in the Lotus* in *The Middle Way*, the journal of the Buddhist Society, London (Vol. 59, No. 1 to Vol. 60, No. 2).

In order to orientate the reader to the welter of diverse terminology employed by the different translators of the texts in the anthology, I have compiled an extensive glossary, which appears at the end of the book.

Among all the people who have kindly assisted in making the compilation of this book possible I would especially like to thank Gyatso Tsering, Director of the Library of Tibetan Works and Archives, Dharamsala; Joshua Cutler; Ven. Ngawang Samten Chophel; Shambhala Publications, Inc; and Snow Lion Publications.

STEPHEN BATCHELOR
Sharpham
1986

Part One
Introduction

I   *The Advent of Buddhism*

One of the chief obstacles to an appreciation and understanding of the Buddhism of Tibet is the aura of mystery which still surrounds it. The notion of Tibet continues to conjure up images of a remote and snow-bound country somewhere in Central Asia, with access to its spiritual life as forbidding as any attempt to cross its earthly frontiers. Amidst those uninviting yet strangely alluring landscapes of barren plains and towering peaks, we sense the presence of red-robed Lamas engaged in unknown rituals; of fearful demons engulfed in haloes of fire; of pacific, multi-armed divinities smiling beatifically; of imposing mountain monasteries which seem to grow out of the rock itself; of yaks and abominable snowmen; of the Dalai Lama; of deeply resonating horns and gongs, cymbals and ceremony. The people who greet us from photographs either stare at us in unkempt bewilderment or retreat from us into an elaborate and ornate backdrop of brocade and symbolism. We sense a peculiar mixture of wild, scarcely tamed passion and exquisitely detached refinement.

This surface impression of Tibet has given rise to a great deal of curiosity and the popular imagination has adopted it as the setting for some of its most improbable fantasies.

Many books, both serious and otherwise, have served to strengthen this impression by reporting mysterious anecdotes and providing accounts of strange doctrines and rituals. Yet however appealing this popular conception of Tibet may be and no matter how much of it can actually be verified, it nevertheless obscures far more than it reveals.

This is particularly true in the case of the form of Buddhism practised in Tibet. All the colourful and exotic imagery that baffles the mind at the very thought of Tibetan Buddhism is simply the outer packaging for a spiritual tradition which in many respects is quite sober, rational, precise and systematic, and one of the most profound and extensive religious systems in existence. Thus, in approaching the teachings of Tibetan Buddhism we should not allow ourselves to be dazzled by what initially meets our eye. Yet this is not to say that the strange and evocative images which the religion presents have no meaning beyond that of exciting the imagination of a devout mountain people. The ferocious deities and solemn rituals have a quite definite meaning; but this meaning can only be fully grasped by understanding the inner dynamics of the religion of which the rituals are but an external expression.

So instead of starting our exploration of Tibetan Buddhism with what has already been impressed upon us by the popular image of Tibet, let us try to get to the heart of the religion and then work progressively outwards. In this way, by understanding the inner world of Tibetan Buddhists, we will slowly be able to appreciate the outer forms in which their spiritual life and values have come to express themselves.

THE BEGINNINGS OF TIBETAN BUDDHISM

Tibetan Buddhism originated in the Buddhist traditions of India. Although many of the ways in which it has been formulated and organized are the product of later Tibetan developments, the main current of the religion can be clearly seen to flow from Indian sources. Much of what informs the consciousness of the Tibetan Buddhist, then, is derived from the way presented in the teachings of Shakyamuni and his followers in India. As such, the basic view of the world in Tibetan Buddhism is that of ancient India, as interpreted from a Buddhist perspective. To understand the foundations of Tibetan Buddhism we must therefore understand the inner and outer spiritual worlds of the Buddhists who lived in India until the twelfth century AD.

Buddhism began to be formally introduced into Tibet from India during the reign of King Songtsen Gampo (617 – 98). Although Buddhist scriptures and religious objects had reached the country as early as 433, it was not until the time of Songtsen Gampo that a concerted effort was made to establish Buddhism as a national religion, to build temples and translate texts. Apart from a brief but violent period of persecution at the beginning of the tenth century under the rule of the anti-Buddhist king Langdarma, Buddhism continued to grow in strength without serious interruptions. One of the most notable periods of its initial development was under King Trisong Detsen (790 – 844). During his reign numerous Indian masters were invited to teach in Tibet; the first Tibetans received ordination as monks; and an unprecedented amount of translation was done by Tibetan scholars working in conjunction with Indian pandits.

Prior to the dissemination of Buddhism, Tibet existed at a fairly primitive level of cultural development. The prevailing religion was a blend of animistic and shamanistic beliefs collectively known as 'Bon.' There was apparently no written form of language and thus no recorded literary or historical documents. Until the second century BC the country was not unified and consisted of a number of warring feudal principalities and tribal groups. It was sparsely populated and had little contact with the outside world. Many Tibetans lived a nomadic existence and there were very few established townships or trading centres.

Yet, surrounding the country to the south and the east were the two most highly developed civilizations of Asia, those of India and China. Tibet's sheer geographical isolation, however, initially prevented it from sharing in the cultural developments of these countries. Even during the period when Buddhism was being transmitted from India to China, Tibet was bypassed. Instead of taking the more direct route across the mountainous regions of Tibet, travellers between India and China found it far easier to take the longer overland route through what is now Afghanistan and the central Asian countries to the north of Tibet. Alternatively, they would travel back and forth by sea. Thus, although it is possible that the Tibetans were to a certain extent influenced by some of the cultural and religious developments of their neighbours, none of these apparently ever took firm root in the country before the formal advent of Buddhism.

One can say, then, that with the introduction of Buddhism, Tibet also received its introduction to high culture. Unlike China, which already had a sophisticated culture and civilization of its own by the time it took an interest in Buddhism, Tibet imported Buddhism as the very basis for all its further cultural developments. In order to translate the Buddhist scriptures, the Tibetans were first obliged to create a written form for their language and to construct a system of grammar. This task was primarily accomplished by the gifted Thonmi Sambhota, a minister of King Songtsen Gampo. He went to India and eventually produced an alphabetic script modelled upon a North Indian form of Sanskrit. He also compiled the first texts on Tibetan grammar, which even today form the basis for any study of the subject.

The Tibetans' translations therefore did not have to make use of terms already weighed down with the ingrained philosophical connotations of indigenous traditions. Nor did their renderings of the Indian Sanskrit have to convey anything but the Buddhist connotations of the original terms. In this way they were able to produce a written version of the Buddhist scriptures which conveyed an exceptional degree of clarity and directness. This task of translating almost the entire written corpus of a highly developed religion into a written language which had barely been invented did not, understandably, proceed without difficulties. During the reign of King Ralpachen (866 – 901) the methods of translation had to be standardized and everything translated up to that date was then revised. Many texts were translated several times and only found an accepted form after several generations of scholars and translators had checked and reworked them.

The initial process of establishing Buddhism in Tibet lasted for about four hundred years (c. 700 – 1100). During this time many Tibetans travelled to India, both to receive instruction and training as well as to learn Sanskrit in order to continue the work of translation. Likewise, many Indian teachers made their way to Tibet and further spread the teachings of Buddhism. When all of the translated material finally began to be collated and organized into an official 'canon,' it included about two hundred and twenty volumes. (The exact number varies according to the different editions.) More than one hundred of these volumes contained the discourses attributed to the historical Buddha. These were collectively titled the 'Kangyur,' which means the 'translation of the word.' The remaining volumes, called the 'Tengyur' – the 'translation of the *shastras*' – incorporated nearly four thousand commentarial works written by Indian masters since the time of the Buddha. In addition, numerous explanatory works were composed by the Tibetans themselves, resulting in what is today one of the most extensive collections of Buddhist literature in any language.

Nevertheless, the sheer quantity and diversity of teachings contained in the Indian Buddhist tradition made it a very difficult and complex task for the Tibetans to reach a clear and integrated understanding of everything recorded in the canon. Indian Buddhism consisted of several different approaches – both in terms of practice and philosophical outlook – to the teachings of the Buddha. Thus it became a primary concern of many of the early Tibetan Buddhist masters to organize these diverse doctrines and practices in a way which could be readily understood by the Tibetan people. In many cases they would base their systematic presentation of Buddhism on earlier attempts at synthesis found in the Indian texts. In other cases, particularly when it came to harmonizing the tantric teachings with the common doctrines of the *sutras*, they had to construct new synthetic models capable of embracing the entire scope of Buddhist theory and practice.

In their presentation of Buddhism, then, the Tibetans did not diverge greatly from their Indian forerunners in terms of doctrinal content but in the ways in which they organized this content into systematic stages leading to enlightenment. It is the logic of the Buddhist path which is Tibetan, not the individual doctrines or insights which are arranged in the light of this logic. What gives Tibetan Buddhism its own peculiar flavour, therefore, is not any uniquely Tibetan ingredient, but the way in which these common Buddhist ingredients have been blended together in the Tibetan mind.

2 *The Path to Enlightenment*

The teachings of Tibetan Buddhism are primarily concerned with elucidating the stages on the path to enlightenment. Yet, implied within these teachings is an entire view
of the world and of our place within it, which was largely
drawn from the traditional Indian conceptions of the universe. Since the Buddhist teachings were explained solely in
terms of this cosmological framework, it was likewise
necessary for the Tibetans to incorporate its features into
their own way of thinking.

TIBETAN BUDDHIST COSMOLOGY

The world as envisioned in this cosmology is one comprised of numerous realms of existence. The earth on which
human beings live is seen as a large triangular continent
situated in an ocean to the south of a tall and majestic moun-
tian called Sumeru. This mountain is like a huge, multi-
levelled, four-sided pyramid which reaches far beyond the
clouds into the heavens. Each side of the mountain is made
of a different precious substance. The side facing the continent where we live is formed of lapis lazuli. Thus, as the sun
makes its daily course around the ocean, its light reflects the

colour of the lapis, causing our sky to appear blue.

Located at the various levels of Mount Sumeru are many different realms of celestial beings. At the lower levels are found the *asuras*. Although the asuras share many of the attributes of the higher celestials, they suffer from the torment of jealousy of those celestials more fortunate than themselves. Thus they find themselves in frequent conflict and strife with them. The celestials at the higher reaches of Sumeru, however, live long and contented lives. While alive, they are subject to neither great physical nor great mental sufferings. Yet when death approaches and they are faced with the prospect of losing their happy condition, they experience extreme misery. Beyond these sensuous celestial planes are found two further planes of celestial existence: those of pure form and formlessness. Here dwell a wide range of celestial beings absorbed in various degrees of concentration. Yet, though their lifespan is even longer and more contented than that of the celestials of the sensuous plane, they are still subject to the suffering of death and continued rebirth.

On the earth and below it are found three other realms in which life is characterized by varying degrees of suffering. These are the animal realm, which includes all land creatures, birds and fish; the *preta* realm, comprised of various ghosts and spirits who live a shadowy and deprived existence; and the different hell regions in which beings are continuously subjected to a wide range of physical and psychological agonies. It is believed that the majority of sentient beings in the universe dwell in these three unfortunate realms of existence and only relatively few have the good fortune to be born in the three higher realms – of human beings, asuras and the higher celestials.

From the traditional Buddhist viewpoint, these different realms are not disconnected spheres of existence. After death in one life-form it is certain that one will take birth again either in the same or in a different realm, according to the force of one's accumulated actions (*karma*). That which continues from one life to the next is a subtle stream of mental consciousness which is said to be both beginningless and endless. Thus, this present life as a human being is seen as a very short-lived event in the overall context of one's continuous existence as a sentient being. In the same way, this present world is regarded as a mere fragment of an infinitely larger universe.

We should keep in mind the outline of this cosmology in order to fully understand the world in which the Tibetan Buddhist lives. Although someone conditioned to view the world through the eyes of the natural sciences might balk at the notion of such a universe and at best treat it as some kind of symbolic map of the psyche, for Tibetan Buddhists it has a very definite reality. The Buddhist teachings, which for Tibetans are the source of this world view, are as authoritative for them as the scientific descriptions of the universe are authoritative for the modern world.

THE STAGES OF THE PATH

One of the very first stages on the path to enlightenment involves the cultivation of an awareness of the spiritual value of human existence in contrast to the spiritual possibilities present in the other realms. We are taught to repeatedly reflect upon the immense good fortune of being born a human being. For among all the various forms of life, it is only as a human being that we have the opportunity to derive the fullest benefit from the teachings of the Buddha. Such an opportunity is regarded as exceedingly rare and, if we do not make good use of this chance now, it is highly unlikely that we will find such an opportunity again for myriad lifetimes. The purpose of this reflection is gradually to produce a conscious awareness of the rarity and value of a human life such that we will be inspired to make the fullest use of its spiritual potential.

Having become aware of the value of our unique human life, we are then taught to realize how utterly transient that life is. We are instructed to reflect repeatedly upon the inevitability of death, the utter uncertainty of the time of our inevitable death, and the fact that only by applying the teachings will we be able to have any control over our destiny after death. The aim of this contemplation is to make us realize that even though we are now a human being, it is imperative to apply ourselves to a spiritual practice lest death overtake us and cast us back into the maelstrom of other possible life-forms within the universe.

Once an awareness of the preciousness yet frailty of human life has been instilled within us, the next stage of contemplation is to carefully consider the disagreeable and miserable character of the three unfortunate realms of existence. By bringing to consciousness the torments of those beings, as well as the possibility of our own rebirth in such realms, we develop a determination to avoid such a fate by all means possible. In this way our mind turns either towards the ways of continuing to be born as a human being in our future lives or else assuring ourselves of rebirth in one of the celestial realms.

Thus we are led to reflect more deeply upon the law of karma which governs the destinies of those living in this universe. Tibetan Buddhist texts describe in detail the psychological mechanisms which give rise to a karmic act; the different consequences of our actions; as well as the means whereby we can evaluate any particular deed ethically. By making ourselves familiar with all these details of the process of ethical causation, we find ourselves in a stronger position to follow a course of behaviour which will result in a favourable rebirth and turn us away from the danger of falling into the unfortunate realms.

The Buddhist teachings as explained in the Tibetan tradition aim at leading us progressively towards an increased awareness of our position and destiny in the universe as well as to a greater understanding of the means whereby we can gradually gain control over this destiny. Once a basic ethical direction has been established for our lives through the preceding reflections, we are then instructed to conscientiously devote ourselves to the threefold Buddhist refuge: the Buddha, the Dharma and the Sangha. By placing our trust in these three 'Jewels,' we are given a sound supportive framework in which to bring our spiritual concerns to their ultimate fulfilment. Through establishing confidence in the Buddha, we accept the authority of one who is fully enlightened about the nature of the universe as well as about what is beyond the universe; through practising the Dharma, we adopt a way of thought and conduct founded upon the teachings of the Enlightened One; and by relying upon the Sangha (ordained ones), we are given the care and guidance of those men and women who are firmly established on the path of Dharma.

One of the more notable characteristics of the Tibetan Buddhist conception of refuge is that in addition to the Three Jewels, which are the source of refuge for all Buddhist traditions, there is added a fourth refuge, namely, the Lama. 'Lama' is a term which has given rise to considerable confusion. It is often thought to be merely the title common to any Tibetan Buddhist monk. In fact it is the Tibetan equivalent of the Sanskrit 'guru,' which simply means 'spiritual teacher.' Hence 'Lama' is the title given to someone who is sufficiently trained in the theory and practice of Buddhism to be in a position to guide others. It is not even necessary for the Lama to be a monk. Some of the most renowned Lamas in the history of Tibetan Buddhism have been unordained lay men and women.

In the practice of Tibetan Buddhism a great deal of importance is given to the role played by the Lama. The teacher who imparts to us the knowledge of the Buddhist path and the means to practise it is regarded as performing the very function of the Buddha himself. Any progress that we are able to make along this path can be traced to the kindness of the teacher who initially showed us the path. Without a spiritual teacher, who has in turn been instructed by his teachers, who have in their turn received instruction from a lineage of teachers going back to the Buddha, it is impossible to gain any living access to the wisdom of the Buddhist tradition. For this reason, the Lama is frequently compared to the Buddha and in many respects considered to be even more significant for our actual spiritual practice than the historical figure of Shakyamuni. Thus, when Tibetan Buddhists recite the formula of refuge, they first take refuge in the Lama before proceeding to take refuge in the Buddha, Dharma and Sangha.

As soon as we accept the specifically Buddhist outlook on life entailed by the act of commitment to the objects of refuge, we are led to view the universe in the light of the Buddha's understanding. It now becomes clear that no matter where we are born within the various realms of existence, there will be no final release from suffering. Even rebirth in the highest formless realm of the celestials is bound to come to an end and we will again have to take birth elsewhere. For this reason Buddha described the destiny of the inhabitants of this universe as 'cyclic' (*samsara*). Propelled by the force of their good and bad deeds, they continue to go round and round from one realm to another without ever finding any lasting peace or happiness.

The next stage on the path to enlightenment is that of renunciation. This entails the recognition not only of the suffering character of existence but also of the causes for such suffering. The most evident of these causes is the force of karma itself, which relentlessly drives us from one realm of being to another. But at the source of karma lies the intention to act; and at the root of this intention lie the impulses of desire for what is pleasurable and aversion towards what is unpleasant. And if we look even deeper, we find that the impulses of desire and aversion are only present because we do not understand the true nature of existence. Hence, renunciation serves as the basis for adopting an entirely new approach to life: one that perseveres in uprooting ignorance, desire and aversion altogether in order to be freed from the vicious chain of events that they invariably set in motion.

METHODS OF CONTEMPLATION

Before continuing with the remaining stages of the path, it would be worthwhile to consider the methods of contemplation employed by Tibetans in order to cultivate the states of awareness which have been described so far. The insight belonging to each stage of the path, be it the insight into the preciousness of human life, the terrible misery of the lower realms, or the need for renunciation, is first approached analytically. Students are given a methodical explanation of the reasons which support such an insight as well as the misconceptions which habitually hinder it. They are instructed to memorize the key points of the explanation and then to systematically contemplate their meaning. This they are expected to do daily as formal meditation while seated in the crosslegged position. The more these points are reflected upon and examined from different angles, the more they begin to penetrate and have an effect upon the way we view our life and the world. As the contemplation progresses we reach a stage where the insight sought will become increasingly more of a natural attitude rather than a contrived idea. At this point it is no longer necessary to continue analyzing the subject intellectually. From now on we should try to concentrate our entire attention on the dawning state of awareness itself. If the strength of this attention declines, then we can briefly run through the points of the contemplation again in order to re-establish the awareness being nurtured within. Through the force of concentration the insight is progressively refined and strengthened until it becomes firmly embedded within consciousness.

Thus the Tibetan Lamas often speak of two phases in the cultivation of meditative awareness. The first phase is that of 'analytical meditation.' Here we repeatedly reflect upon the object of meditation and seek to validate it through

reasoning and inference. The second phase is that of 'concentrated meditation.' At this stage we cease to think con-
ceptually about the object and instead place the full force of
our concentration upon the very state of awareness which
has been generated through the analytical reflection. In this
manner the thinking process is used as a basis for reaching a
concentrated state of awareness in which the discursive
faculty of thought finally falls away of its own accord.

3 Compassion

The principal form of Buddhism which has prevailed in Tibet has been that of the Mahayana – the 'Great Vehicle.' Central to this tradition is the emphasis given to the qualities of compassion, loving kindness and the altruistic resolve to realize enlightenment for the benefit of others (*bodhicitta*). The Mahayanists also developed a view of the Buddha which was not wholly centred around the historical figure of Shakyamuni. They were conscious of numerous Buddhas and bodhisattvas whose function it is to symbolize the various aspects of the Buddha's enlightenment. Although, on one level, these beings are treated as objects of devotion and supplication, on a deeper level they are understood to be personifications of various states of consciousness – qualities to be cultivated within ourselves through meditation.

AVALOKITESHVARA – THE BODHISATTVA OF COMPASSION

Included in the Tibetan pantheon are literally hundreds of such Buddhas and bodhisattvas. Yet among all of these figures the Tibetans undoubtedly hold Avalokiteshvara, the Buddha of compassion, closest to their hearts. Avalokiteshvara, or Chenrezig as he is known in Tibetan, also appears in a variety of forms and aspects. The most common is that of a seated, four-armed bodhisattva. His body is radiant white, he is clothed in flowing robes with the skin of a deer over his left shoulder; in the two hands which are clasped at his chest he holds a jewel; his other two hands are raised to shoulder level, the right one holding a crystal rosary and the left a lotus flower; his head is adorned with a diadem of five jewels; he is surrounded by an aura of light; and he sits upon a white moon disc supported by a lotus throne; as the personification of the Buddha's compassion he smiles kindly and gently on all beings.

The special affection the Tibetans have for Avalokiteshvara is even reflected in the myths of their pre-history. According to legend, Avalokiteshvara once appeared in the world as a monkey king. This monkey king was a devout lay Buddhist who decided to go to the mountains of Tibet in order to practise meditation. While he was in a cave meditating he was observed by a local demoness who fell in love with him. To make him return her affection, she appeared one day in the form of a beautiful woman. The monkey king initially refused to be seduced by her, until she threatened to devour every being in the country unless he married her. He finally consented and they had six children, each being reborn from one of the six different realms of existence.

At first the family lived on the wild fruits that grew in the area but soon their supply of food ran out. To prevent his children from starving, the monkey king requested Avalokiteshvara for assistance. At his behest Avalokiteshvara caused an abundance of crops to grow throughout the land. By living on these crops, the monkey-demon children began to shed the fur from their bodies and to lose their tails. Finally they stood upright, as human beings. From them descended the Tibetan race. It is said that the Tibetans' temperament is related to their two original forebears. From the monkey king they inherited the qualities of diligence, kindness and an interest in religion, and from the demoness a tendency to be short-tempered, passionate and jealous.*

THE MEANING OF MANTRA

There are many ways of entering into a spiritual relationship with Avalokiteshvara, and of developing the qualities of mind he represents. By far the most common of these is the recitation of the mantra OM MANI PADME HUM. This mantra is to be found on the lips both of the simplest peasant and the most erudite doctor of metaphysics. Many Tibetans say it under their breath almost incessantly, often to the accompaniment of the perpetual clicking of prayer beads. The individual syllables are often inaudible; instead, the prayer becomes a rhythmic humming sound which pervades the workplace and the household, the mountain path and the monastic cloister.

Etymologically, the word 'mantra' means 'to protect the mind.' The repetition of a mantra such as OM MANI PADME HUM becomes a device for keeping the mind focused on a specific spiritual theme – in this case the quality of the Buddha's compassion as personified by Avalokiteshvara. In this way the mind is 'protected' against the usual influx of unwholesome and disturbing thoughts. Thus protected, one finds a certain degree of inner calm and is able to keep one's mind in a greater state of awareness and concentration.

Depending upon the capacity of the individual, the function of the mantra OM MANI PADME HUM can be understood in different ways. Fundamentally, it is seen as a form of supplication to an external deity residing in a distant paradise. By constantly reciting the mantra it is believed that Avalokiteshvara will protect one against material hardship

*Adapted from Geshe Wangyal, *The Door of Liberation,* pp. 33-44.

and sickness, and that one establishes a bond with him which will cause one to be reborn in his Pure Land after death. At a deeper level the mantra is recognized as a means of turning one's mind towards the cultivation of compassion. For, in the final analysis, Avalokiteshvara is nothing but compassion and, as such, is latent within the minds of all living beings, waiting to be brought to full actuality. Thus, in many of the more advanced practices related to Avalokiteshvara, one seeks primarily to identify oneself with the deity rather than seeing him primarily as an externally existent force or being.

The meaning of the individual words and syllables of the mantra is also subject to numerous interpretations. In one practice, for example, each of the six syllables – OM-MA-NI-PAD-ME-HUM – is associated with one of the six realms of existence. Each syllable is given a specific colour, which is correlated with the symbolic colours of each realm. As one recites the mantra, one imagines innumerable rays of light shining out from each syllable and illuminating the beings of the particular realm with which that syllable is associated. In this way one extends the practice of the mantra into an awareness of every realm of life, thus weakening any self-centred motives one might have had in reciting it. Moreover, this radiating light is considered to symbolize the boundless compassion of Avalokiteshvara for all those who are subject to suffering. The recitation of the mantra thus becomes far more than just the faithful repetition of a prayer. It can be seen as a symbolic act which aims at an integrated spiritual orientation in relation to the world in which one lives.

Another way of interpreting the mantra would be to consider the symbolic meaning of each word. OM is an ancient mystic syllable with a long history in the spiritual life of India. The Tibetans, from a Buddhist standpoint, frequently explain its function at the beginning of a mantra as the initial evocation of the perfectly unified body, speech and mind of the Buddha. The second word, MANI, is the Sanskrit term for 'jewel'; and the third, PADME, the Sanskrit for 'lotus'. The symbolic meaning of the jewel and the lotus can be understood on a number of levels. However, in the context of Mahayana Buddhism, they refer first and foremost to the two principal themes of the path to enlightenment: method (*upaya*) and wisdom (*prajna*). Method, symbolized by the jewel, includes all those aspects of the path which are founded upon a compassionate concern for others. These include generosity, ethical conduct, forbearance, compassion itself, and loving kindness. Wisdom, symbolized by the lotus, refers to the inner qualities of tranquillity and insight through which enlightenment into the true nature of reality is gained. The final syllable, HUM, symbolizes the five aggregates (*skandha*) which in Buddhism have traditionally been regarded as the basic constituent elements of the person. In the state of enlightenment, however, these five aggregates are transformed from their present defiled condition into the five Dhyani Buddhas, that is, five corresponding yet purified aspects of Buddhahood.

According to this interpretation, the mantra OM MANI PADME HUM functions as a symbolic and highly condensed expression of the entire path to enlightenment. It serves to remind one that this path is one of process and transformation. It indicates how, through applying the practices of method and wisdom, one can progressively transform oneself from a being fettered to the cycle of birth and death into a Buddha whose mind is freed from this cycle yet whose words and deeds continue to stream forth compassionately for the benefit of others.

Although this mantra can serve as a means of focusing the mind upon the qualities of Avalokiteshvara and the nature of the path which can lead to his state, its effectiveness depends upon the degree to which we have actually internalized this path within ourselves. The mere recitation of the mantra is incapable by itself of ever producing any of the qualities of method and wisdom. It is necessary that these qualities be systematically cultivated through specific reflections and meditation.

HOW TO DEVELOP COMPASSION

In addition to being the characteristic feature of the method aspect of the path, compassion is also the foundation for Mahayana Buddhism as a whole. Thus, the importance of Avalokiteshvara does not lie merely in his personification of a single quality of the Buddha's mind, but in his embodiment of the very driving force of the Mahayana practice. In order to actually develop this quality of mind within ourselves, the Tibetan masters teach a number of different contemplations. As a preparatory basis for compassion it is first of all necessary to rid the mind of the grossest forms of attachment and aversion towards others. This entails cultivating a state of equanimity in which the habitual biases and prejudices that mar our relationships are evened out.

As a means of developing this balanced state of mind, we are instructed to imagine three different people in front of us: a good friend, a personal enemy, and someone to whom we are indifferent. Then we should consider each of these people in turn and examine the nature of our feelings towards them. In each case we will discover that the way in which the three people appear is largely determined not by any inherent qualities of theirs but by the subjective manner in which we have chosen to view them. By rigidly classifying this person as a 'friend,' this one as an 'enemy' and the other as a 'stranger,' we impose barriers to appreciating the basic humanity which unites them all. Equanimity is thus developed by training ourselves to see the fundamental equality of all beings which lies behind the self-imposed veil of differences.

The next stage in this reflection is to recognize that, in addition to being essentially equal, other beings are also essentially kind towards us. This recognition can arise out of the awareness that throughout our innumerable past lives we have always been dependent upon the kindness of a mother to give birth to us and rear us. Since our previous births have been countless, it is probable that at one time or another, every other sentient being has been a mother to us. Starting with the example of the mother we have in this life, we should recollect in detail the personal hardships and self-sacrifices she has undergone for our sake. Once we are strongly aware of her kindness, we should then recall that *all* beings have at one time demonstrated such selfless concern towards us. As we continue to practise this contemplation, the sense of others as having been as kind to us as our own mother in this life should gradually increase and come to overrule any conflicting feelings of dislike or indifference.

When a recognition of the essential kindness of others is firmly established in the mind, we will then become conscious of the fact that we are indebted to them for what they have done for us. And in considering the miserable state in which all of them are now imprisoned by their defiled impulses and deeds, there should now arise in us the same feelings towards them as we would have for our own mother were we to see her subjected to suffering. Such feelings would consist of the earnest longing to free them from their torment and the wish to be able to grant them happiness. In this way compassion – the intention to separate others from their suffering – and loving kindness – the intention to give them happiness – are born in the mind.

The following stages of this contemplation aim at discovering the means for actually realizing the goal of compassion and loving kindness. We should first observe that both the means and the goal of compassion are invariably dependent upon our conception of the nature and origins of the other person's suffering. If our awareness of suffering is primarily one of physical illness, for example, then we will regard the cure of such illness as our goal and the proper treatment of the causes of the illness as the means. Now, in the context of the Buddhist view of life described here, the extent of suffering cannot be limited to certain physical or mental disorders experienced in this life alone. For suffering is the very nature of cyclic existence and thus cannot be eliminated unless we uproot the deeply embedded mental impulses and karmic potencies which relentlessly keep us bound to the cycle of repeated birth and death. It follows that for a Buddhist the goal of compassion and loving kindness cannot be fully realized until these causes of cyclic existence itself have been completely removed.

By means of the preceding stages of the contemplation, we extend the range of our compassionate concern to include all sentient beings regardless of whether they are friends, foes or strangers. Tibetans often use the expression 'all mother-like sentient beings' to emphasize the sense of gratitude and indebtedness we should feel towards others. As this compassion for the suffering of all beings grows, we become increasingly aware of the extent and depth of the suffering experienced within the realms of existence. And so the enormity of the task of even alleviating a fraction of this misery becomes apparent. Yet, in order to be true to the compassion and loving kindness spontaneously growing within our hearts, we are led to the seemingly impossible idea of taking it upon ourselves to strive for the eradication of suffering in its totality. This attitude of resolve is called the 'supreme intention.' With this intention one grasps the ultimate goal of compassion and loving kindness: the freedom of all beings from every form of suffering and their achievement of lasting well-being.

It now remains to consider what would be the most effective means for actually realizing this lofty aspiration. It is clearly necessary that, in order to be in a position to lead others out of suffering, we should have found freedom from suffering ourselves. It would be impossible for us who have not succeeded in untying the knots of our own confusion to untie the knots of our neighbour's. Thus, the initial prerequisite for achieving the goal of compassion is to eliminate within ourselves what we aspire to eliminate within others. From a Buddhist standpoint this would entail the removal of all defiled mental impulses and karmic traces by the systematic application of ethical conduct, concentration and wisdom. But merely to be free from these things ourselves is not sufficient in itself to enable us to effectively work towards the elimination of these factors within others. As well as striving to liberate ourselves from the bondage of cyclic existence, therefore, it is equally necessary to cultivate the skills of communicating with and working for the welfare of others.

The optimal development of these two faculties of liberating wisdom and liberating method is found only in the state of Buddhahood. For a Buddha is one who has found liberation from suffering through his or her wisdom into the nature of reality, yet is still fully active within the realms of existence working for the liberation of others. Hence, the most effective means of realizing the supreme intention is to aspire to attain Buddhahood oneself and to set out on the path which leads to that goal. The state of mind infused with such an aspiration is known as the 'mind of enlightenment' (*bodhichitta*). And once this attitude becomes uncontrived and spontaneous one is said to enter the path of the bodhisattvas, that is, those beings whose lives are dedicated to achieving enlightenment for the sake of all others.

4 *Wisdom*

The function of wisdom within our minds is to enable us to break free from the cycle of birth and death. The reason it is able to do this is because it is the very antidote to what keeps us locked into the cycle of repeated birth and death – that is, ignorance. Ignorance causes us to experience ourselves and the world in which we live in a way which does not conform to their reality. A person whose mind is clouded by ignorance is similar to someone in a darkened room confusing a length of rope with a snake and becoming gripped by fear. Ignorance 'darkens' the clarity of the mind, leads us into confusion and error, and sparks off a chain reaction of disturbing emotions. Just as a person who is terrified by the imagined dangerous snake is driven to all kinds of irrational actions, so does the person who is intellectually and emotionally confused by ignorance behave unrealistically and impulsively. It is in this way that the mechanism of cyclic existence is established. Confusion leads to irrational actions; irrational actions lead to unpleasant and frustrating experiences; such experiences continue to confuse the mind, and so on. When extended to the context of birth, death and rebirth, this cyclic movement propels us endlessly from one realm of existence to another.

In order to undo this confusion, and thus to halt the chain reaction of irrational behaviour and suffering which it sets in motion, wisdom enables us to understand the self and the world in the way they actually exist. This process of understanding is one that takes place on a number of levels and at varying degrees of intensity. In one sense every stage along the path involves the cultivation of a certain amount of wisdom, for whenever a misconcepton about an aspect of reality is dispelled, wisdom emerges in its place.

Wisdom has as its objects both relative and ultimate truths. However, release from the confusion which lies at the root of cyclic existence is only gained by penetrating to the ultimate truth of oneself and the world. Each of the major schools of thought transmitted from India to Tibet developed its own characteristic understanding of what constituted this ultimate truth and how it differed from truths which were merely relative. Although all of these understandings stemmed from scriptures attributed to the Buddha, they nevertheless differed considerably from each other; there are long records of the debates and arguments which these schools had engaged in to defend their own positions and to refute the assertions of the others. Thus, the Tibetans inherited several well-formulated Buddhist philosophical systems as well as a great deal of polemical literature to support each school. Subsequently, within Tibet itself, certain movements were made towards the further development of Buddhist philosophy, but for the most part the Tibetans remained within the framework of philosophical thought and speculation already established by their Indian predecessors.

Traditionally, Tibetans consider there to be four principal schools of Buddhist philosophy: the Vaibasika (literally: Vaibasa-follower), the Sautrantika (literally: Sutra-follower), the Chittamatra (Mind-only) and the Madhyamika (Middle Way). The first two of these schools are usually considered to be representative of the Hinayana tradition and the latter two as representative of the Mahayana.

Although the Tibetans study all four systems of thought, for practical purposes it is the philosophy of the Sautrantika, Chittamatra and Madhyamika which are given the most attention.

As the basis for his philosophical and doctrinal training, a Tibetan monk will often be instructed first in the Sautrantika. Much of this instruction is taken up with the careful definition of terms, the study of logic and the art of debate, as well as an explanation of the main principles of epistemology. Although these subjects are taught within a Sautrantika frame of reference, their usefulness extends far beyond their application to the Sautrantika philosophy alone. This training in logic, debate and epistemology forms the foundation for all subsequent philosophical enquiry. And so, many years are often spent in making sure that the young students have a solid grasp of these subjects. They are learning, in effect, how to master the tools of philosophical investigation, so that later they will be able to advance fruitfully into their studies of the subtleties of Mahayana thought.

None the less, the Sautrantika viewpoint itself is also of considerable importance and needs to be thoroughly learned before one proceeds to the philosophies of the Chittamatra and the Madhyamika. The position taken by this school could perhaps be referred to as one of 'phenomenal realism.' The proponents of the Sautrantika philosophy maintain that ultimate truth consists of whatever is immediately perceptible through direct, non-conceptual cognition. This, for them, includes all data which are evident to sensory perception, such as visual forms, sounds, smells, tastes and tactile sensations, as well as whatever is perceived by the different levels of direct mental perception. Each of these ultimately true phenomena are further characterized as being impermanent, the products of causes and conditions, subject to destruction, as well as causes in their own right. They are regarded as bearing their own substantial reality and as existing independently of any conditioning by subjective or conceptual factors.

Relative truth, according to the Sautrantika school, consists mainly of the mental constructs imposed by people upon the ultimate reality which is immediately perceived through direct cognition. Mental constructs, which include such things as ideas, abstractions and generalities, are characterized as permanent phenomena not involved in the dynamic processes of momentary change and causation. The classic example of a relative truth is the abstract notion of space, defined as 'the mere absence of obstructive contact.' Such a notion of space is not something which is presented to the senses but is construed by the mind on the basis of sensory perceptions and then subsequently imposed on the world of direct experience. Although it is not ultimately real in the way that forms and sounds are ultimately real, such space is nevertheless *relatively* real. Since forms and sounds are observed to travel from one point in space to another, it is correct to infer that there is an absence of obstructive contact, without which they could not move. This abstract space then is a relative truth.

Although these relative truths, which we project upon the raw data of ultimate truths, may tend to obscure a direct, unfiltered perception of ultimate truth, they do not actually contradict it. What really serves to conceal ultimate truth from us are the false mental constructs we have imposed upon it and these do contradict it. There are basically three false mental constructs which distort our perception of reality and thus cause ourselves and the world to appear in a way in which they do not exist. The first of these is the idea of permanence which we erroneously project upon what is in fact impermanent; the second is the idea of satisfactoriness which we project upon what is unsatisfactory; and the third is the idea of self which we project upon what is selfless. All of these three deeply-rooted ideas are in complete opposition to the reality of ultimate truths, which are fundamentally characterized as impermanent, unsatisfactory and selfless.

In order to gain a direct and unobscured perception of ultimate truths it is therefore necessary to dispel from one's mind the erroneous conceptions of permanence, satisfactoriness and self which distort and conceal the impermanent, unsatisfactory and selfless nature of reality. This is the goal not only of the Sautrantika but of all the other Buddhist schools of thought as well. What distinguishes the Sautrantika from the other schools is its description of what actually constitutes ultimate truth, namely that the numerous impermanent, unsatisfactory and selfless phenomena *themselves* are the ultimate truths; whereas in the two Mahayana systems of philosophy such phenomena are regarded only as relative truths.

CHITTAMATRA

The first Mahayana school of thought, the Chittamatra, asserts as its principal doctrine that 'all phenomena are of the nature of mind.' In contrast to the Sautrantika, which maintains that the physical and mental elements of reality have their own independent existence, for the followers of Chittamatra there are no material entities which exist separately from the nature of mind. Everything we experience has its origin in the mind; and the basis of all confusion is the mistaken assumption that mind and matter, subject and object, are two separate and unrelated phenomena. Thus, in addition to dispelling the grosser misconceptions of permanence, satisfactoriness and self, it is necessary to uproot the deeper misconception of externally existing phenomena before we can be finally liberated from ignorance about the nature of reality. For, as long as this notion of the separate existence of mind and matter persists, the root of all other misconceptions will still remain within us.

The Chittamatrins maintain that the ultimate truth is the non-duality of subject and object. To perceive this non-duality is to dispel the misconception that mind and its objects are two separate substances. The adherents do not deny that matter, that is non-mental phenomena such as forms, sounds, smells, etc., exists. They only deny that it exists separately from the substance of mind. For example, when we look at a table, it seems to us that our perception of the table is one thing and the table is something completely different and unrelated to it. In reality, however, the table and the perception of the table are inseparable and originate from a single source within the mind, neither being more nor less 'real' than the other. It is only the habitual force of ignorance which makes us cling to the idea that they are separate.

Relative truth, then, encompasses all impermanent phenomena, such as the constituents of the apparently external world and all mental states, as well as the validly constructed ideas and abstractions which are imputed to those phenomena. We, and the universe in which we live, therefore, fall into the category of relative truths. Yet by positing the ultimate truth of these phenomena to be a state of nonduality in which they are seen to stem from a single source of mind, our habitual notion of the nature of ourselves and the universe changes. All the different realms of existence, for example, can no longer be thought of as external physical regions existing apart from the minds of those beings who experience them. In the Chittamatra philosophy, the distinction between what is 'outside' and 'inside' the mind is purely relative. Ultimately, nothing separates them. Everything in the universe can be accounted for by understanding the nature of the mind alone.

MADHYAMIKA

The second of the Mahayana schools is Madhyamika. As the name 'Madhyamika' (Middle Way) itself suggests, the aim of this philosophy is to reveal a perception of reality which sees things from a viewpoint free from extreme positions. According to this school, both the Sautrantika and the Chittamatra standpoints are too extreme and are unable to effectively defend themselves against critical analysis.

The Sautrantika view of reality exhibits a number of weaknesses, and by exposing them the Madhyamika questions the credibility of the entire system. The first of the weaknesses is the attribution of ultimacy to the individual phenomenal components of reality. If forms or sounds or mental states really possessed such ultimacy, then this ultimate identity should become clearer the closer one examines the phenomenon in question. But once subjected to such analysis, every physical or mental entity can be broken down into numerous parts and the sense of any ultimate identity becomes more and more tenuous. Even the parts themselves can be further dissected into atoms or moments which, in turn, can be mentally analysed *ad infinitum*.

The second major flaw in the Sautrantika position is its failure to acknowledge the role played by the mind in contributing to the appearance of reality. Is it really possible, for example, to have any knowledge of a table independently of the idea 'table' which has been formed in the mind? Could we ever demonstrate the existence of something as entirely separate from all the linguistic and conceptual devices we use to apprehend it? By pursuing such questions, the Madhyamika attempt to show that the Sautrantika vision of reality – that there are numerous independently and objectively existing elements – is difficult to uphold.

In turning their critical analysis to the tenets of the Chittamatra school, the Madhyamika philosophers likewise uncover a number of questionable points. Although the Chittamatrins are conscious of the role of mind in the creation of reality, they can be criticized as having over-exaggerated its significance. For them, mind becomes the sole reality to which all other phenomena can be ultimately reduced. Thus, they tend to ascribe to it a similar kind of independent and ultimate existence as the Sautrantika ascribe to their elements. Such a notion of mind is suspect since it implies that the existence of mind can be established independently of any objects appearing to it. In this case it would contradict the most characteristic feature of mind, namely, the fact that mind is invariably conscious *of* something. And surely it would be self-contradictory to speak of a state of consciousness which is not conscious of anything.

To arrive at its central tenet, the Madhyamika begins with a systematic critique of all positions which show a tendency to extremism. Characteristic of all forms of extremism is the temptation to consider what one believes in as having an ultimate validity and substantiality which exists independently of all other conditions. For the Madhyamika, though, all that can ever be said to have any claim to ultimacy is the very impossibility of an ultimate and intrinsic identity itself. The absence of such a mode of being is technically called 'emptiness' (*shunyata*). Yet even this emptiness is not regarded as having any independent or intrinsic identity, so that although the Madhyamika consider it to be the ultimate truth, it should never be thought of as bearing any characteristics of ultimacy.

Generally speaking, whatever is acknowledged in the world as being real is regarded as a relative truth. Since people have agreed to believe that objects with certain characteristics are tables and that tables are different from whatever goes on in the mind, then such descriptions are relatively true. But as soon as these objects are subjected to a more probing analysis designed to uncover what is really the case with them, the criterion of common sense can no longer be appealed to. As one searches for the 'real' table among its parts or tries to establish that the table exists independently of consciousness, one finds that the web of assumptions which seems to hold the world in place starts to collapse. Finally, one discovers that there is nothing with an ultimate and indestructible identity residing at its innermost core; and that there is no such thing as a table which exists independently of the consciousness which conceives of it as such.

This brief account of Buddhist philosophy necessarily only covers some of the more salient points. A monk in the Tibetan tradition who decides to dedicate himself to doctrinal study can spend twenty years or more before gaining mastery of the subtleties of Buddhist thought. In addition to learning the tenets and approaches of the main philosophical schools, he must also study such subjects as the structure of the various paths to enlightenment, the details of Buddhist phenomenology (*abhidharma*), and the rules and regulations of monastic discipline (*vinaya*) in depth.

As the scriptural basis for these studies, the Tibetans primarily refer to commentarial works compiled by native scholars. They also consult Indian commentaries but rarely make a detailed study of the sutras themselves. They feel that the content of the Buddha's discourses is most clearly expressed through the commentarial tradition, whereas initially to try and make one's way through the complex and contradictory volumes of the sutras themselves would lead the beginner into further confusion. The commentaries are regarded as a key to unlock the treasures concealed within the sutras. The first task of doctrinal study, therefore, is to acquire this key. Once it has been obtained, students should have the confidence to steer their own way through the intricacies of the sutras.

MEDITATIVE WISDOM

The final goal of Buddhism cannot, however, be realized by doctrinal study or philosophical enquiry alone. Such a course of training can serve to cultivate the kinds of analytical wisdom derived from study and logical investigation, but is incapable of freeing one from the innermost bonds of cyclic existence. This is the task of meditative wisdom.

Study and enquiry can be a stepping stone to this wisdom but can never be a substitute for it.

The Tibetan approach to developing meditative wisdom follows two main courses, according to the different abilities and inclinations of individuals. Those who are intellectually orientated are encouraged to cultivate first a clear analytical understanding of the nature of ultimate truth as explained in Buddhist philosophy. In this, most Tibetan traditions adhere to the Madhyamika view. Some, however, incorporate elements from the Chittamatra system and others have evolved their own original interpretations of these two main schools of thought. Once a firm intellectual insight has been attained, students are then instructed in the methods for developing single-pointed mental quiescence (*shamatha*). The goal is to unite their analytical insight with the power of quiescent concentration, thus enabling them to apply their insight at the deepest levels of consciousness. Moreover, through the force of sustained concentration, the analytical character of their understanding diminishes and finally ceases. In this way they achieve a direct, non-conceptual vision of ultimate truth capable of eradicating the ingrained habits and tendencies of ignorance.

People who are not inclined towards lengthy intellectual analysis are taught to cultivate wisdom in a number of different ways. Often this entails starting with the development of mental quiescence and then, when the mind is calm and firm, proceeding to apply either a simple line of reasoning or another means aimed at directly penetrating the ultimate truth concealed behind the veils of obscuring thoughts and emotions. Two of the best-known methods for achieving such insight are found in the teachings of the Great Seal (*mahamudra*) and the Great Completion (Tib., *dzog-chen*). These are both very direct methods for realizing the fundamental nature of mind, and are often taught in conjunction with certain tantric practices.

5 *The Tantras*

Tibetan Buddhism is often seen as just a form of Tantrism where whatever Buddhist teachings were introduced from India soon became assimilated into the native shamanist religion. These assumptions are being corrected nowadays by the growing volume of reliable literature on Tibetan Buddhism, but there still persists considerable confusion about the origins and role of tantric practices in Buddhism.

It should be clear from the preceding chapters that fundamentally Tibetan Buddhism is firmly rooted in the tradition of classical Indian Buddhism. The view of the world and the purpose of human existence are determined neither by 'Tantrism' nor by indigenous Tibetan conceptions, but by classical Buddhist ideas. Moreover, the tantric teachings themselves are not merely the product of the local culture but originate from India. Many of the major tantric texts are translations from Sanskrit and the lineages of tantric practice can be reliably traced back to Indian masters.

The Tibetans, as did their Indian forerunners, insist that the tantric teachings were initially taught by Buddha himself. Like the Mahayana doctrine which maintains that enlightened beings are capable of simultaneously issuing numerous manifestations of themselves, the Tibetans believe that Shakyamuni manifested in various forms and delivered esoteric teachings to select groups of disciples. The tantric teachings of the Buddha were subsequently kept alive either by the efforts of small groups of adepts passing on their wisdom from one generation to the next or else were kept safe in certain non-human realms until human beings became sufficiently advanced to bring them back to earth and disseminate them more widely.

PADMASAMBHAVA

Undoubtedly, the father of Tantric Buddhism in Tibet was the Indian adept Padmasambhava. As his name indicates, Padmasambhava is reputed to have been born in the form of a lotus blossom. Some claim that he took birth eight years after the death of Shakyamuni in what is now northern Pakistan, and through his tantric powers lived for more than a thousand years. Many Tibetans also believe he is still alive in the land of the Rakshas and can be encountered by those with a high level of spiritual attainment. He came to Tibet during the ninth century at the invitation of King Trisong Detsen. His specific task at that time was to subdue the demonic forces which were obstructing the building of Samye, the first major monastery in Tibet. Having defeated these forces he travelled throughout the country teaching the Mahayana and tantric doctrines as well as subduing other local demonic influences which were hindering the spread of Buddhism.

By exercising the powers derived from tantric practice, Padmasambhava was able to challenge the native shamanist priests on their own ground and appeal directly to a level of spirituality which was deeply rooted in the Tibetan religious consciousness. His 'subduing' and 'conversion' of anti-Buddhist 'demonic forces' can be understood as breaking the hold of the shamanist deities on the minds of the Tibetans by introducing them to the higher and more universal truths of Buddhism. But unlike the scholars of Buddhist doctrine and philosophy he did not present the values of Buddhism in a purely conceptual form but revealed them as embodied in living symbolic forms.

Padmasambhava's presentation of Buddhism through the medium of tantric deities and forces struck a very sympathetic and receptive chord within the minds of the Tibetans. The subsequent widespread popularity of tantric practice can probably be attributed to the innate spiritual disposition of the Tibetans to respond more readily to religious truths that are embodied and personified. In this way the teachings of Buddhism came alive for the Tibetans and ceased to be mere abstract ideas and doctrines. But most notable about the Buddhism of Tibet are the ways in which the non-tantric and tantric teachings have been unified into a systematic whole. Each of the major Tibetan schools has succeeded in producing a synthesis of the Buddhist path which incorporates both of these seemingly diverse trends inherited from India.

The Sanskrit word *tantra* refers mainly to the texts in which the tantric teachings are recorded. So when the Tibetans use the term tantra they usually do so as a way of distinguishing a certain body of Buddhist literature – the tantras – from the other major works in the canon, the sutras. 'Tantrism' and 'Tantric Buddhism' are terms coined by modern writers and have no precise equivalents in the Tibetan language. In Tibetan the most common designation for the teachings and practices recorded in the tantras is 'secret mantra' (*guhyamantra*). And the path to enlightenment that includes the practices taught in the tantras is referred to as the 'diamond vehicle' (*vajrayana*).

THE FOUR DIVISIONS OF TANTRIC PRACTICE

The tantras are included in the Kangyur, that is, the canonical literature attributed to Shakyamuni, and they have been classified into four main sections. Each section contains a number of treatises, all of which describe a certain level of tantric practice. The four sections are: the Action Tantras (*kriyatantra*), the Performance Tantras (*charyatantra*), the Yoga Tantras (*yogatantra*), and the Supreme Yoga Tantras (*anuttarayogatantra*). Although the doctrines of all four tantras have been preserved in Tibet, in actual practice the Tibetans concentrate primarily on the teachings of the Action Tantras and the Supreme Yoga Tantras. Moreover, in the Nyingma school one also speaks of the three inner tantras – Maha Yoga, Anu Yoga and Ati Yoga – rather than the Supreme Yoga Tantras.

These four (or six) sections of tantric teachings are primarily graded according to the type of relationship one establishes with a deity. Here the word 'deity' (*deva*) is used in a completely different sense from that of either Judaeo–Christian or Hindu theism. It refers to the luminous beings who personify and embody particular qualities of Buddhahood. The purpose of tantric practice is to progressively integrate these enlightened qualities into one's own consciousness. This is achieved by establishing a rapport with the deity, such that one's insight into the qualities symbolized by him or her gradually deepen and become one's own.

THE ACTION TANTRAS

In the practice of the Action Tantras, one concentrates on cultivating a relationship with a deity who is conceived as having an identity separate from one's own. One learns to visualize the deity in the space before one, to contemplate the qualities of mind he represents, to make various prayers, praises and offerings to him, to recite his mantra, and finally to imagine that he dissolves into light and is absorbed into one's own body, speech and mind. The best-known deities of this class of tantra are Avalokiteshvara, Manjushri, Vajrapani, Vajrasattva and Tara. They symbolize respectively the compassion, wisdom, power, purity and enlightened activity of Buddhahood.

The Action Tantras describe a state in which one's own impure and defiled condition is contrasted with the pure and undefiled being of the deity. By establishing a relationship with the deity and gradually absorbing the qualities he represents, one seeks to progressively rid oneself of defilement and to reach his state. In the practices of the Supreme Yoga Tantras, however, the initial relationship one establishes with the deity is radically different. Here one completely identifies oneself with the deity, and one's abode with his Pure Land. One has to discard all thought of oneself as being in any way distinct from the deity, to the point of cultivating the pride that one *is* the deity. In such practices one trains oneself to regard everything one does as the activity of a fully enlightened Buddha. This method of training, which is unique to the Supreme Yoga Tantras, is known technically as 'taking the three Bodies of the Buddha as the path.' In other words, instead of seeing Buddhahood as a distant goal, one strives to realize Buddhahood within every phase of one's present existence.

The final aim of such tantric practice is to achieve a union with the deity such that one's mental, vocal and physical expressions spontaneously reflect the enlightened state of a Buddha. To actualize this union is equivalent to the attainment of Buddhahood itself. Thus the various phases of identification with the deity simply describe the special tantric approach to realizing enlightenment. The end result of Buddhahood, as with the progressive cultivation of compassion and wisdom, is no different from what is described in the Mahayana sutras. The difference between the teachings of the sutras and the tantras does not lie in the nature of the goal but in the nature of the methods employed to realize that goal. And it is on this point that the Tibetans generally consider the tantric teachings to be superior to the doctrines of the sutras: tantric methods are said to enable practitioners to achieve the result of Buddhahood far more swiftly. For this reason the diamond vehicle (Vajrayana) is sometimes called the 'swift path.'

THE STAGES OF PRACTICE WITHIN THE SUPREME YOGA TANTRAS

Nevertheless, this swift path is no easy short-cut to enlightenment. It involves a rigorous training which requires the utmost of the practitioner. One must be prepared to adhere to a strict code of ethical discipline and undergo lengthy and arduous preliminaries before one can even start to practise the initial stages of identification with the deity. In addition to having cultivated the fundamental qualities of renunciation, an altruistic resolve of bodhichitta and a certain level of insight into ultimate truth, one is required to perform a set of five preliminary practices. These are: (1) offering one hundred thousand full-length prostrations; (2) reciting the hundred-syllable mantra of Vajrasattva one hundred thousand times; (3) taking refuge in the Triple Gem one hundred thousand times; (4) making one hundred thousand symbolic offerings of the universe; and (5) reciting the mantra of one's personal Lama one hundred thousand times. The purpose of these five preliminaries is to strengthen one's resolve and faith in the tantric practices and to help eliminate the tendencies in one's mind which would hinder such practice.

The preliminaries completed, it is then necessary to be formally initiated into the mandala of a particular deity. 'Initiation' is a process of empowerment in which one receives permission from a qualified tantric preceptor to engage in the practice. One sees the preceptor as an embodiment of the deity in question. Although mandalas are usually depicted as circular, symmetrical designs, they are in fact merely simplified, two-dimensional diagrams of the actual mandalic realm. The true mandala is an immense sphere at the very centre of which the deity resides in a palace. The entire mandala is the manifestation of the deity's wisdom and is inseparable from his state of enlightenment. It is a transparent and luminous world in which every detail symbolizes a facet of Buddhahood.

The first principal stage of the Supreme Yoga Tantra

practice of identifying oneself with the deity is to completely dispel from one's mind the ordinary images and ideas one has of oneself and the world. This is achieved by learning to see and think of oneself as the deity and the world as his mandala. To achieve this transformation of one's ordinary perceptions and thoughts requires the sustained recollection of every detail of both the deity and the mandala. Starting from the purified expanse of emptiness, one must repeatedly train oneself to create, detail by detail, the form of the deity and the mandala. Every shape and colour needs to be fixed firmly in the mind's eye until it seems so real that one feels one could actually reach out and touch it. Then one has to be able to dismantle this universe piece by piece. The outer regions of the mandala progressively dissolve into the inner regions, which, in turn, dissolve into the deity. The deity is then gradually absorbed into the centremost point at his heart which finally collapses into emptiness again.

In addition to transforming the habitual images of oneself and the world, this practice of repeatedly creating and dissolving the form of the deity and the mandala also serves to strengthen one's concentration and imagination. Yet no matter how real one may feel this new identity to be, it nevertheless exists only through the force of concentrated imagination. Although one has succeeded in generating the outer form of an enlightened being and his world, it still remains to imbue this form with the actual dynamics of enlightenment. Hence, this first phase of tantric practice in which one constructs the form of the deity and the mandala is called the 'stage of generation' and the final phase, in which Buddhahood is actually realized within the context of this form, is known as the 'stage of completion.'

One of the most distinctive features of the teachings expounded in the Supreme Yoga Tantras is their understanding of the threefold structure of body and mind. According to these doctrines, there exist gross, subtle and extemely subtle levels of both body and mind. The gross level corresponds to the physical form of the body and the normal waking state of consciousness; the subtle level refers to the energies of the body prana, their channels (*nadi*) and points of juncture (*chakra*), and the dream state of consciousness; the extremely subtle level is an indestructible drop of energy (*bindu*) located at the heart, and the consciousness present during deep sleep. In the sutras the practice of Buddhism is largely restricted to the gross level of physical existence and waking consciousness. But in the tantras, and especially during the stage of completion, one strives to continue one's practice at both the subtle and extremely subtle levels of body and mind as well.

This stratified conception of physical and mental existence found in the tantras also qualifies the traditional Buddhist understanding of the relationship between body and mind. Only at the gross level are mind and body now considered to be significantly different and separate phenomena. At the subtle level mind is seen as distinct yet inseparable from physical energy. Wherever there is mind or consciousness, there will invariably be found a subtle physical energy accompanying it as its 'driving force.' And at the extremely subtle level, mind and body are regarded as essentially identical. Thus, in essence mind and body are understood as a singular phenomenon and only by becoming progressively grosser do they begin to exhibit increasing differences and seeming incompatibilities.

This view of body and mind sheds further light on the processes of death and rebirth. The three levels of physical and mental existence are analogous to the phases of death, the intermediate period between death and rebirth (Tib., *bardo*), and the stage of being born into a particular realm; during a single twenty-four hour cycle, the mind and body pass through a series of phases which are basically similar to these processes. Falling into a state of deep sleep in which all consciousness and physical energy is withdrawn into the heart is similar to death; coming out of deep sleep and dreaming is similar to the intermediate period; and waking up to the consciousness of the external world and the gross physical body is similar to rebirth. In both cases the same pattern of dissolution and regeneration can be observed. During death and deep sleep only the extremely subtle unified level of body and mind is functioning; during the intermediate period and dreaming the body and mind operate only on the subtle level; and during rebirth and waking consciousness the gross divided level of body and mind becomes evident.

In contrast to the traditional Mahayana theory, the tantras present a radically new interpretation of the doctrine of the three Bodies of the Buddha. According to the traditional Mahayana, these three Bodies (*kaya*) represent the three principal aspects of Buddhahood. The Dharma Body (*dharmakaya*) is the all-pervasive and fundamental spiritual core of enlightenment; the Enjoyment Body (*sambhogakaya*) is the subtle, ethereal manifestation of the Buddha which dwells in a Pure Land and is only directly accessible to highly advanced bodhisattvas; and the Emanation Body (*nirmanakaya*) is the physical manifestation of the Buddha which appears in the realms of existence. The tantric teachings, however, recognized that these three Buddha Bodies can also be related to the three levels of body and mind and the threefold process of death, the intermediate period and rebirth. In contrast to the somewhat metaphysical interpretation of the Mahayana sutras, the tantric adepts realized that the same pattern of dissolution and regeneration that underlies deep sleep, dreaming and waking as well as death, the intermediate period and rebirth, is likewise at work behind the Dharma Body, the Enjoyment Body and the Emanation Body.

The aim of tantric practice, therefore, is to transform the defiled and unsatisfactory processes of deep sleep, dreaming and waking, and death, the intermediate period and rebirth into their purified aspects of, respectively, the Dharma Body, Enjoyment Body, and Emanation Body. The notion of attaining Buddhahood no longer involves, as it does in the sutra teachings, first rejecting the forces which drive the cycle of birth and death, then realizing the transcendent state of the Dharma Body, and finally issuing Enjoyment Body and Emanation Body manifestations back into the cycle of existence. For the very process of dissolution and regeneration which now leads one through the experiences of death, the intermediate period and rebirth is essentially the same as that which allows the Dharma Body to assume the aspects of the Enjoyment Body and the Emanation Body. Even the forces of desire and hatred, which according to the sutras are to be utterly eliminated, are realized in the tantras to be merely gross manifestations of subtler levels of energy and consciousness. And as such they need not be denied: the point is to grasp their neutral energetic nature and reconstitute it as a wholesome quality of mind.

The difficulty, of course, is that we normally have no consciousness of or control over the functioning of the subtle and extremely subtle levels of our physical and mental activity. Thus, during the stage of completion one is taught a number of methods for consciously activating the subtle and extremely subtle levels of mind and energy through the force of meditation. Yet, before one can even begin these practices it is essential to have mastered the imaginative concentration developed by creating and dissolving the form of the deity and his mandala during the stage of generation. Only through the power of this concentration will one gain the ability to effectively activate and then transform and redirect the physical and psychic forces operating at the subtle and extremely subtle levels of one's being. The stage of generation is, in a sense, like a dress rehearsal for enlightenment. It is a precise, symbolic enactment of the transformation of the processes of death, the intermediate period and rebirth into the Dharma Body, Enjoyment Body and Emanation Body of a Buddha. The stage of completion which follows it can be compared to the actual performance of the play.

In order to activate the subtle and extremely subtle levels

of consciousness, practitioners who have advanced to the stage of completion must engage in a number of practices in which they learn to control the energies of the body. These practices are especially important for the activation of the extremely subtle level of body/mind – the deepest seat from which all other mental and physical functions originate. To achieve this goal it is necessary to consciously collect and dissolve all the energies and mind states of the gross and subtle levels into the indestructible drop located at the heart. This procedure is analogous to what occurs at death.

Once the extremely subtle level of body/mind has been activated, it is necessary to transform it from its neutral state into a concentrated awareness of ultimate truth. In this way the practitioner establishes the basis of the Dharma Body and, in tantric terms, achieves a state of intimate union with the deepest levels of the deity's mind. The subsequent phases of the practice correspond to the natural re-emergence of the subtle and gross levels of mental and physical activity. As the subtle level emerges, one reassumes the luminous form of the deity and his mandala. This is the Enjoyment Body aspect of Buddhahood which is the transformed state of the ordinary dream and intermediate period levels of existence. Finally, returning to the gross level of materiality and waking consciousness, one arises in the Emanation Body aspect of Buddhahood, thus completing the process of transformation and achieving a state of union with every facet of the deity.

When aspiring to engage in the practices of one of the Supreme Yoga Tantras one must first seek out a teacher qualified and willing to initiate one into the mandala of a particular deity. According to their own disposition, as well as on the advice of the teacher, the student may be initiated into the practices of one of numerous deities. Some of the more common of these deities are Guhyasamaja, Chakrasamvara, Yamantaka, Mahakala and Vajrayogini. Once they have received the initiation, they may be required to contemplate daily a text which describes the deity and the mandala, thus reminding them of the form and goal of the practice. But in order to dedicate themselves seriously to the practices of the stages of generation and completion, it is necessary to enter into a strict meditational retreat. These retreats can be undertaken either alone or with a small group of fellow practitioners. They are frequently designed to cover a period of three years, three months and three days, during which time the practitioner goes through the whole cycle of practices associated with a particular deity.

6   The Buddhocracy

The extent to which Buddhism came to influence the social, cultural and political life of Tibet was unparalleled elsewhere in Asia. Apart from the short period of repression under Langdarma, Buddhism remained the unquestioned spiritual authority of the land from the time of King Songtsen Gampo in the seventh century until the recent Chinese usurpation of power in 1959. During this time thousands of monasteries flourished; vast numbers of men and women entered the religious orders; shrines, reliquaries and religious inscriptions were evident in every corner of the country. The three largest monastic institutions around the capital Lhasa resembled small townships, each of them with a population of more than five thousand monks. It has been estimated that during this time one out of every three men in the country was a monk.

Buddhism was initially able to establish itself as the national religion owing to the enthusiastic patronage of the early kings – especially Songtsen Gampo and Trisong Detsen. Unlike in other Asian countries, where the demise of a ruler often meant a change in religious sympathies, in Tibet the patronage of Buddhism continued despite the break-up of subsequent dynasties. Such was the strength of

Buddhism in the land that it gradually came to dominate not only the religious life of the people but the political climate as well. In 1253 the powerful Mongolian Emperor Kublai Khan appointed his Tibetan religious adviser Drogön Chögyal Phagpa as supreme political authority over the whole of Tibet. Phagpa was a monk of the Sakya school of Buddhism; and during the century that followed Tibet continued to be ruled by representatives from this tradition. This was probably the first example anywhere of a Buddhist monk's assuming the position of head of state.

THE DALAI LAMA

In 1349 the Sakya dynasty was overthrown and for the next three hundred years the country was ruled by a succession of secular kings. The last of these kings was finally deposed by another Mongolian ruler, Gusri Khan, in 1642. As a means of securing the stability and unity of Tibet, the Mongolian conquerors then appointed Ngawang Lobsang, the fifth Dalai Lama (1617 – 1682) as ruler of Tibet. The Dalai Lama was also a monk and he belonged to the influential Geluk school, which had been founded two hundred and fifty years previously by Tsongkhapa. The rule of the Dalai Lamas and the political power of the Geluk tradition lasted for more than three hundred years, until 1959. The present Dalai Lama, His Holiness Tenzin Gyatso (b. 1935) is the fourteenth in this lineage.

The institution of the Dalai Lama is a peculiarly Tibetan phenomenon in which political pragmatism and Buddhist metaphysics are interwoven. The first in the line of Dalai Lamas was Gendun-drup (1391 – 1474). He was a monk and one of the closest disciples of Tsongkhapa. The successive Dalai Lamas, however, were neither elected nor appointed from among a number of qualified contenders for the post. Instead, following the death of a Dalai Lama, his followers would set out to search for the baby boy as whom the deceased Dalai Lama had reincarnated. Once it was confirmed by a number of tests, oracular consultations and so forth that this boy was indeed the reincarnate Dalai Lama, he would be taken to Lhasa and rigorously trained from this early age to assume his responsibilities as both the secular and spiritual ruler of Tibet.

However extraordinary this system of continuity of power may initially appear, it makes perfect sense in the light of the Tibetan Buddhist view of life and the world. In a universe where rebirth is a fully accepted fact and where Buddhas and bodhisattvas deliberately manifest for the benefit of others, why should an advanced practitioner of the Mahayana not be able to reincarnate in a form which is of special benefit to the people of a particular country? Further credibility is added to this claim if one considers that the bodhisattva in question has been trained in the tantric practice of actually transforming the ordinary taking of rebirth into the Emanation Body of a Buddha. The status and quasi-divinity of the Dalai Lama are underlined by the fact that the Tibetans consider him to be a manifestation of Avalokiteshvara.

The idea that once a teacher had died and taken rebirth one could then seek out, recognize and reinstate him in his former position neither originated with nor was exclusively applied to the Dalai Lama. In Tibet there were hundreds of lines of reincarnated spiritual teachers. Such a teacher is usually referred to as a *tulku*, which is the Tibetan term for the Emanation Body. Most sizeable monasteries in the country would have a *tulku* as their spiritual leader. And each major school would normally be led by a reincarnate teacher.

As Buddhism spread and became established in Tibet a number of different schools came to be formed. Most of these were founded on the teachings and personality of either a Tibetan or Indian master who had introduced a certain line of thought and practice from India. During the course of their development later disciples of these founding figures organized their doctrines into a more cohesive and comprehensive whole until they began to assume an internally consistent mode of expression. There finally emerged four major Buddhist traditions, each with its own distinct lineage of teachers and clearly discernible manner of presenting the Dharma.

NYINGMA

The first school to develop was the Nyingma. The name means 'the ancient ones' and the school traces its origins back to Padmasambhava. Many of the Nyingma teachings are based on the earliest translations of the Buddhist scriptures made during the eighth and ninth centuries when the religion was first introduced to Tibet. The Nyingma also rely on certain scriptures (called *terma* or 'treasure texts'), composed and hidden by Padmasambhava, and rediscovered at various times by *terma* discoverers (*tertons*). Characteristic of the Nyingma teachings is their ninefold classification of the path to enlightenment. The first three of these paths, called the 'causal vehicles,' are those described in the different sutras. And the remaining six paths, called the 'resultant vehicles,' are those taught in the various tantric texts. The two most important teachers to further elucidate the Nyingma doctrines were Longchen Rabjampa (1308 – 1363) and Jigme Lingpa (1729 – 1798).

All the schools which subsequently came to be formed based their teachings on later translations of the sutras and tantras. These traditions can be collectively called the 'new schools' because of their reliance on these new translations. In this way they are generally distinguished from the 'old school' of the Nyingma.

Three of these new schools arose during the highly active and creative eleventh century. They were the Kadam, the Sakya and the Kagyu schools. The Kadam tradition was founded by the Indian master Atisha (982 – 1054) who came to Tibet in 1042. Atisha and his disciples emphasized the need for a solid foundation to the basic insights of Buddhism as a prerequisite for engaging in the more advanced tantric practices. Although this school was most influential in clarifying the order and perspective of the Buddhist path to enlightenment and produced a number of renowned teachers, it was absorbed into the other schools and did not survive for very long as an independent tradition.

SAKYA

The Sakya tradition was founded by Könchog Gyalpo (1034 – 1102) who established a monastery in the Sakya region of south-west Tibet in 1073. Könchog Gyalpo had travelled to India and studied under an Indian master named Gayadhara. The principal doctrine he received was that of 'The Path and its Fruit,' a teaching of the ninth century adept Virupa which unified the different teachings of the sutras and the tantras. After Könchog Gyalpo the Sakya tradition was further developed by the so-called 'five venerable masters' who flourished during the twelfth and thirteenth centuries. It later divided into two sub-sects, the Ngor and Tsar traditions, under the influence of Ngorchen Kunga Zangpo (1382 – 1457) and Tsarchen Losal Gyatso (1502 – 1565).

KAGYU

The third school to emerge during the eleventh century was the Kagyu tradition founded by Naropa, Marpa and Milarepa. Naropa (1016 – 1100) was a renowned Indian tantric master who had previously been a great scholar and dialectician. The Tibetan translator Marpa (1012 – 1099) travelled to India to receive Naropa's teachings which he then transmitted to his main disciple Milarepa (1052 – 1135). The founders of this tradition were mainly concerned with the experience of Buddhism as realized through tantric practice and were wary of becoming sidetracked by the intellectual and academic abstractions which frequently beset the Buddhist theoreticians of their time. Milarepa's chief disciple was Gampopa (1079 – 1153), a monk who had originally studied with Kadam teachers. Through him the school received the additional influence of the teachings of Atisha and his followers. From Gampopa are derived the four major sub-schools of the Kagyu tradition.

GELUK

More than two hundred years were to elapse before the next major school of Tibetan Buddhism was founded. This was the Geluk tradition established by Lobsang Drakpa, a monk from the Tsongkha region of eastern Tibet, who came to be known as 'Tsongkhapa' (1357 – 1419). The Geluk school was to a large extent an eclectic reform movement which sought to re-establish the original Indian foundations of Buddhism. Although Tsongkhapa studied widely under teachers from all the different schools of his time, he derived his main inspiration from the teachings passed on to him from the Kadam tradition and its founder Atisha. Throughout his writings he emphasized the need for a thorough training in the doctrines of the sutras before progressing to the practices of the tantras. The Geluk tradition eventually developed into the largest school in Tibet and, once the Dalai Lama was enthroned as ruler of the country, came to wield a great deal of political power.

These schools differ from one another more in their emphasis, presentation, terminology and interpretation than in any substantial element of content. As with religious groups everywhere, though, the history of their co-existence has been marked by a certain number of ongoing disputes. Each school claims to have a special lineage of teachings or a system of doctrinal interpretation, the very exclusiveness of which are sometimes invoked to indicate a certain superiority over the other schools. Yet although these disagreements have occasionally erupted into acrimonious and even violent conflicts, they have been balanced by an emphasis on unity and non-sectarianism which has been evident in the teachings of many of the greatest masters from all the main traditions.

As suddenly as Tibet had opened its gates to welcome the doctrines of the Buddha, so did it shut them again once those teachings were firmly secured within its borders. Once their basic doctrines had been introduced from India, the different Tibetan schools took it entirely upon themselves to preserve and further elucidate them. In the subsequent development of Tibetan Buddhism no other external influences were instrumental in modelling the character of the religion. The Tibetans seem to have been entirely unaffected by the teachings of the T'ien-t'ai or Hua-yen schools, the two great doctrinal traditions which flourished across the border in China. Neither were they aware of the commentarial tradition founded by Acharya Buddhaghosa, prevalent in the Theravada schools of Sri Lanka and South-East Asia.

Yet the most remarkable instance of the Tibetans' resistance to other forms of Buddhism is found in their reaction to the attempted introduction of the Ch'an (Zen) school from China during the eighth century. A Chinese monk called Hva Shang had come to Tibet from T'ang China and was expounding the doctrine of sudden enlightenment in the tradition of Hui Neng. His growing popularity began to disturb King Trisong Detsen, who was currently engaged in spreading the teachings of Indian Buddhism, which tended to emphasize a graduated and progressive approach to enlightenment. To resolve this apparent contradiction, the King invited the famous scholar Kamalashila from India to hold a formal debate with the Chinese teacher Hva Shang. The debate was held at Samye monastery outside Lhasa with the King presiding. After each participant had stated his point of view and tried to defend himself against the critique of the other, Kamalashila was declared the victor. Hva Shang was duly despatched back to China and the King issued a decree which, in effect, outlawed the doctrines and practices of the Ch'an school in Tibet.

From the middle of the seventeenth century, when the Dalai Lama was installed as head of state, until the middle of the twentieth century Tibet underwent very little change. A policy of isolation was followed which discouraged any further spiritual or cultural interchange. The sheer geographical inaccessibility of the place prevented all but the most dedicated Christian missionaries from entering the country, and these, in any case, were notably unsuccessful in gaining any converts. The major Buddhist schools continued to produce a succession of highly-trained scholars and meditators. The faith of the common people remained strong; numerous commentarial works were composed; and the practice of the religion was kept very much alive. But apart from the non-sectarian 'Ri-me' movement, which arose around the turn of this century, no other schools were to emerge.

When the forces of the modern world began to encroach on the borders of Tibet, the country found itself completely vulnerable and almost defenceless. The Tibetans discovered that they had tried to construct an ideal system in a far from ideal world. And now this world at large, which had previously been ignored by the Tibetans and had likewise shown little interest in Tibet, discovered that it had a number of reasons for interfering in its affairs. Many of these reasons were geopolitical in nature. Tibet was seen to occupy a strategic position between a number of ideologically hostile powers. And as the world came to be divided into the present spheres of influence, Tibet found that it lacked the military strength, political know-how and international connections to resist being gradually swallowed up by a larger neighbour.

During the early decades of this century the thirteenth Dalai Lama (1876 – 1933) realized the precarious condition of his country and tentatively began to introduce a number of reforms. After his death, however, most of these were cancelled by the conservative elements among the monks and aristocracy who feared that any modernization would endanger the status quo. Internally, the country was weakened at this time by a considerable amount of factional infighting and intrigue. And despite the benevolent intentions of the Dalai Lamas, the feudal system tolerated a level of material underdevelopment which provided the Communist Chinese with a convenient justification for offering their 'assistance' to the Tibetan people.

In the early months of 1959 it became quite clear that the Chinese programme of assistance was merely a pretext for their designs to undermine the Dalai Lama's government and make Tibet part of the People's Republic of China. In Lhasa on March 10th that year a large crowd of Tibetans rebelled against the Chinese, only to be swiftly and forcibly suppressed. The Dalai Lama managed to escape the fighting and fled to safety in India. He was shortly followed by about eighty thousand of his people who chose to be refugees in India rather than to live under foreign occupation in their own country.

During the twenty-seven years since then the Central and Western parts of Tibet have been renamed 'The Tibetan Autonomous Region,' while the eastern districts of Kham and Amdo have been incorporated into the Chinese provinces of Sichuan and Qinghai respectively. The country is now completely under the control of the Chinese. During the cultural revolution of the late 1960s a large percentage of the monasteries and religious sites were destroyed. Monks and nuns were disrobed and religious practices were all but forbidden. Recent visitors to Tibet, however, testify that the Buddhist faith still remains deeply rooted within the people. They have observed that recent relaxations in Chinese policy concerning religion have resulted in a massive outpouring of religious expression among the Tibetans.

The Dalai Lama continues to live in exile in India. The refugee population is now fairly well organized into settlements and communities throughout India, Nepal, Sikkim and Bhutan. A number of Tibetans have emigrated abroad, notably to Switzerland, Canada and the United States. Each of the four major schools has managed to build several monasteries and continues to ordain and train young monks and nuns. During the last decade a considerable number of centres and institutes have been founded in Europe, America and Australia by Tibetan Lamas for the purpose of training foreigners in the doctrines and practices of Tibetan Buddhism. The future of Tibet, the Tibetan people and Tibetan Buddhism cannot be foreseen. But it is not easy to imagine that the only Buddhocracy the world has known will ever be restored to what it once was.

Part Two
The Kadam Tradition

Essential Advice of the Kadampa Masters

This Kaliyuga is not the time to display your ability; it is the time to persevere through hardship. It is not the time to take a high position, but the time to be humble. It is not the time to rely on many attendants, but the time to rely on isolation. Nor is it the time to subdue disciples; it is the time to subdue yourself. It is not the time of merely listening to words, but the time of contemplating their meaning. Nor is it the time to go visiting here and there; it is the time to stay alone.

Atisha

Introduction to Part Two

This short text is a compilation of dialogues, words of advice and reflections of most of the major figures in the Kadam tradition. The first third of the text is devoted to the teachings of Atisha, the Indian founder of the school. It continues with instructions given by his foremost Tibetan disciple Drom. Finally, the text records the sayings of a dozen other teachers from the lineage.

The teachings of the Kadampa masters are noted for their straightforwardness, their almost uncompromising simplicity. These masters continually confront us with the basic facts of our existence and challenge us to adopt a meaningful and practical response to them. They repeatedly point out that the spiritual path is fraught with as many possibilities of self-deception as is our life in the world. To avoid such pitfalls we must be constantly mindful of our innermost motives, our aims, our commitments and, most significantly, our death.

This text was first translated into English under the guidance of the Mongolian Lama Geshe Wangyal by some of his American students. It was published as part of a collection of Tibetan Buddhist writings entitled *The Door of Liberation* in 1975. The text presented here is an abridged version, containing about three-quarters of the original.

1 *Advice from Atisha*

When Atisha arrived in Tibet, his three disciples, Ku, Noke and Drom asked him: 'To attain the high state of liberation and omniscience, which is more important, to follow the precept of the Lama or to follow the scriptures and commentaries?'

Atisha replied, 'The precept of the Lama is more important than scriptures and commentaries.'

'Why is that?' they asked.

'Even if you know that the primary characteristic of all phenomena is voidness, and can recite the tripitaka as well, you and the teaching will be completely separate if you do not apply the precept of the Lama at the time of practice.'

Again the disciples asked: 'Please define the practice of the precept of the Lama. Is it simply striving to do virtuous deeds in body, speech and mind, and acting in accordance with the three vows: the vow of individual liberation, the Bodhisattva vow, and the tantric vow?'

'Both of these are insufficient,' answered Atisha.

'But why?'

'Although you keep the three vows, if you do not renounce the three realms of samsara, your activities will only increase your worldliness. Although you strive to perform virtuous deeds in body, speech and mind, both day and night, if you do not dedicate this work to the enlightenment of all, you will end up with numerous wrong concepts. Though you meditate, and are considered a holy and wise teacher, if you do not abandon your interest in the eight worldly concerns, whatever you do will be only for the purposes of this life, and in the future you will not find the right path.'

On another occasion Atisha was asked by Ku, Noke and Drom, 'What is the highest teaching of the path?'

Atisha replied, 'The highest skill is in the realization of egolessness. The highest nobility is in subduing your own mind. The highest excellence is in having a mind which seeks to help others. The highest precept is continual mindfulness. The highest remedy is in understanding the naturelessness of everything. The highest activity is not to conform with worldly concerns. The highest siddhi is the lessening and transmutation of the passions. The highest giving is found in non-attachment. The highest moral practice is a peaceful mind. The highest patience is humility. The highest effort is to abandon attachment to activities. The highest meditation is the mind without pretension. The highest wisdom is not to grasp anything as it appears.'

'And what is the final goal of the Teaching?' the three disciples asked.

Atisha replied, 'The final goal of the Teaching is possession of the essence of voidness and compassion. Just as in the world there is a panacea for all sickness called the solitary heroic medicine, there is the realization of voidness which remedies all the fettering passions.'

'But many say they have realized voidness. Why do their anger and attachment remain?'

'They are speaking empty words, for when you fully realize the meaning of voidness, your body, speech and mind react with pleasure, like slipping fresh butter into barley soup. The great sage Aryadeva said:

> The nature of existence –
> Is it empty or not?
> Merely feeling this doubt
> Tears samsara asunder.

'Therefore, when you realize the correct meaning of voidness, it is just like the solitary heroic medicine, for all the path is included in that realization.'

'How do you include the entire path within the realization of voidness?' the disciples asked.

'All the path is included in the six transcendences (paramitas). When you realize the correct meaning of voidness – and lose your blind lust for all things, material and spiritual – your life becomes one flowing act of transcendent giving. In the absence of attachment, you are no longer defiled by non-virtuous deeds, and you enter the ever-flowing harmony of transcendent moral practice. In this freedom from defilement, you also liberate yourself from the passionate domination of "I" and "mine," and attain the ever-flowing transcendent patience. As you take great pleasure in the realization of voidness, your life becomes one ever-flowing transcendent effort. Through this, you lose all attraction to objects and enter the ever-flowing transcendent meditation. And finally, when your mind is freed from the habit of seeing everything through the prism of three aspects, you will attain the ever-flowing transcendent wisdom.'

'Is it possible for one who realizes the meaning of voidness to attain Buddhahood with only the wisdom and meditation of voidness?' a disciple asked.

Atisha replied, 'Whatever you perceive, whatever you proclaim – there is nothing that has not come from your own mind. Understand that this realization of mind is empty. Understanding the non-duality of the realization of mind and of voidness is *wisdom*. *Meditation* is the continuous concentration on this wisdom without any distraction. *Deeds* are accumulating merit and wisdom while you realize from the viewpoint of this meditation that everything is like an illusion. Once you are under the influence of these three, their practice will come even in dreams. Once it has come in dreams, it will come at the moment of death. When it comes at the moment of death, it will be present in the bardo. Once it is present in the bardo, there is certain to be accomplishment of the superior siddhi, and you will become a Buddha.'

When the venerable Atisha first visited Tibet, he stayed in the western province of Na-ri. He gave many precepts to the assembled disciples who were under the guidance of Hlachang Chubö, and then after two years had elapsed, he decided to return to India. Just as Atisha was departing Hlachang Chubö asked, 'Even now as you are leaving, could we have one more precept?'

Atisha answered 'What I have already taught you is enough.' But Hlachang Chubö persisted in his request, so Atisha gave this precept:

'How wonderful! Dear friends, you have clear realization and great knowledge, while I have small worth and am not very intelligent. Yet, since you who are close friends and dear to my heart request me, I give you this advice from my childish knowledge.

'Friends, until you have obtained enlightenment, the Lama is needed; therefore depend upon the holy spiritual teacher. Until you fully realize the nature of voidness, you must listen to the Teaching; therefore listen closely to the precept of the Lama. Merely understanding the Dharma is not enough to be a Buddha; you must practise constantly.

'Go far away from any place that is harmful to your practice; always stay in a place that is conducive to virtue. Clamour is harmful until you obtain a firm mind; therefore stay in an isolated place. Abandon friends who increase your fettering passions; depend on friends who cause you to increase virtue. Bear this in mind. There is never an end of things to do, so limit your activities. Dedicate your virtue day and night, and always be mindful.

'Once you have obtained the precept of the Lama, you should always meditate on it and act in harmony with his speech. When you do this with great humility, the effects will manifest without delay. If you act according to the Dharma from the depths of your heart, both food and necessities will come naturally.

'Friends, there is no satisfaction in the things you desire. It is like drinking sea water to satisfy thirst. Therefore be content. Annihilate all forms of pretentiousness, pride and conceit; be subdued and peaceful. Abandon all that which some call virtue, but which is really an obstacle to the practice of Dharma. As if they were stones on a narrow slippery path, you should clear away all ideas of gain and respect, for they are the rope of the devil. Like snot in your nose, blow out all thoughts of fame and praise, for they serve only to beguile and delude.

'As the happiness, pleasure and friends you have accumulated are of but a moment's duration, turn your back on them. Future life is longer than this life, so carefully secure your treasure of virtue to provide for the future. You leave everything behind when you die; do not be attached to anything.

'Leave off despising and deprecating others and generate a compassionate mind to those who are your inferiors. Do not have deep attachment to your friends and do not discriminate against your enemies. Without being jealous or envious of others' good qualities, with humility take up those good qualities yourself. Do not bother examining the faults of others, but examine your own faults. Purge yourself of them like bad blood. Nor should you concentrate on your own virtues; rather respect those as a servant would. Extend loving-kindness to all beings as though they were your own children.

'Always have a smiling face and a loving mind. Speak honestly and without anger. If you go about saying many senseless things, you will make mistakes; thus speak in moderation. If you do many senseless things, your virtuous work will cease; give up actions that are not religious. It is useless to make effort in unessential work. Because whatever you do comes as a result of your karma from long ago, results never match your present desires. Therefore be calm.

'Alas, it is far better to die than to cause a holy person shame; you should therefore always be straightforward and without deceit. All the misery and happiness of this life arise from the karma of this and previous lives; do not blame others for your circumstances. Remember to repay the kindness of the Lama, as all happiness is his blessing.

'Until you subdue yourself, you cannot subdue others; therefore, first subdue yourself. As you are unable to ripen others without clairvoyance, make a great effort to achieve clairvoyance.

'You will surely die, leaving behind whatever wealth you have accumulated, so be careful not to gather defilement due to wealth. As distracting enjoyments are without substance, adorn yourself with the virtue of giving. Always keep pure moral practice, for it is beautiful in this life and ensures happiness in future lives. In this world-age of the Kaliyuga, where hatred is rampant, don the armour of patience, which nullifies anger. We remain in the world by the power of sloth; thus we must ignite like a great fire the effort of achievement. Moment after moment your life is wasted by the lure of worldly activities; it is time to meditate. Because you are under the influence of wrong views, you do not realize the nature of voidness. Zealously seek the meaning of reality!

'Friends, samsara is a vast swamp in which there is no real happiness; hurry to the place of liberation. Meditate according to the precept of the Lama and dry up the river of samsaric misery. Always keep this in mind. Listen well to this advice, which is not mere words but comes straight from my heart. If you follow these precepts you will make not only me happy, but yourselves and all others as well. Though I am ignorant, I urge you to remember these words.'

When the venerable Atisha was staying in Yerpadrak, near Lhasa, he gave the following precept to Yeshe Barwa of Ölgood:

'I bow down to the Blessed One and to Arya Tara.
I bow down to the Holy Lamas.

'Noble sons, reflect deeply on these words. In the Kaliyuga lives are short and there is much to be understood. The duration of life is uncertain; you do not know how long you will live. Thus you must make great effort now to fulfil your right desires.

'Do not proclaim yourself a monk if you obtain the necessities of life in the manner of a layman. Though you live in a monastery and have given up worldly activities, if you fret about what you have given up, you have no right to proclaim, "I am a monk living in a monastery." If your mind still persists in desire for pretty things and still produces harmful thoughts, do not proclaim, "I am a monk living in a monastery." If you still go about with worldly people and waste time in worldly, senseless talk with those with whom you live, even though you are living in a monastery, do not proclaim, "I am a monk living in a monastery." If you are impatient and go about feeling slighted, if you cannot be even the least bit helpful to others, do not proclaim, "I am a bodhisattva-monk."

'If you speak thus to worldly people, you are a great liar. You may get away with saying such things. However, you cannot deceive those who have the boundless sight of clairvoyance, nor can you deceive those who have the Dharma eye of great omniscience. Neither can you deceive yourself, for the effects of karma follow after you.

'Moreover, when generating bodhi-mind, remember the vows you have taken before the Lamas and deities. Do not say, "It is too difficult to be patient," when you meet with someone who gives you the opportunity for special patience. Remember that even if it is very difficult, there is always something that can be done. Prior to taking a vow, consider carefully whether it is too difficult for you to keep. For if you do not keep a vow once you have taken it, you will be deceiving the Lamas and deities. And again, always remember that even though a thing seems to be difficult, there is always something that can be done.

'To stay in a monastery it is necessary to give up worldly ways and attachment to friends and relatives. By renouncing these, you are getting rid of all the co-operating causes of attachment and longing. From then on you must seek the precious bodhi-mind. Not even for an instant should you allow your past obsession with worldly concerns to arise. Formerly, you did not properly practise the Dharma, and under the influence of past habits that sapped your strength, you continually produced the concepts of a worldly person. Because such concepts are predominant, unless you make use of strong antidotes to them, it is useless to remain in a monastery. You would be like the birds and wild animals that live there.

'Do not think, "It is too difficult to apply the antidotes right now." If the wish-fulfilling jewel should happen to fall from the hands of a blind man, he may never find it again. As you practise, do not count the months and years, but continually examine the strength of your meditation and the extent of your realization. See whether or not your fettering passions are diminishing. Always be mindful. Do not make yourself miserable, nor should you ever even attempt to deceive yourself or the Lamas and deities. Do not do anything that would bring disaster to yourself or others.

'When you diminish the activities of this life, you are only doing what is necessary. If there is a heap of filth in front of you, you have to get rid of it quickly. Should someone help you, why not be happy? In the same way, you must get rid of all your habitual thoughts, using whatever antidotes are available to you. And, if the Lama and your spiritual friends help you to do this, why not be happy?

'Do not be angry with those who would harm you. If you allow yourself to become angry, how can you meditate on patience? When fettering passions arise, you must remember their opposing practice. Otherwise, why bother with religious practice while increasing fettering passions? Constantly guarding your precious bodhi-mind, you should not have the slightest gap in your remembrance. If even a tiny gap should appear, the devil of fettering passions will enter. And when this devil enters, he will obstruct the bodhi-mind, and you will be unable to help others and even fall into lower states of being. Think it over.

'Even if you have the thought, "I have done religious practice," you will go to death empty-handed. Noble son, when you die, be careful that your Lama and spiritual friends do not worry or despair. Do not bring doubt or despair to lay people who are faithful to the Dharma. You must check yourself again and again by comparing the teaching of Buddha with your own mind. If you do not do this, even though you think, "I have done religious practice," you will stray from the teaching. Because of this, at the time of death there will be no sign of your having practised bodhi-mind and when the sign that you will fall into lower states of being appears, others will feel great anxiety and despair. Therefore, do not be lazy in your practice of the Dharma or let yourself be deceived by the proud thought, "I have spent my whole life devoted to religion," and thus go empty-handed into the instant of death.

'In short, staying in a monastery will not be helpful if you do not reverse your obsession for fine things and do not renounce the activities of this life. For if you do not cut off these inclinations, thinking that you can work for the aims of both this and future lives, you will perform nothing but incidental religious practice. This type of practice is nothing but hypocritical and pretentious practice done for selfish gain.

'Therefore, you should always seek spiritual friends and shun bad company. Do not become settled in one place or accumulate many things. Whatever you do, do in harmony with the Dharma. Let whatever you do be a remedy for the fettering passions. This is *actual* religious practice; make great effort to do this. As your knowledge increases, do not be possessed by the demon of pride.

'Staying in an isolated place, subdue yourself. Have few desires and be contented. Neither delight in your own knowledge nor seek out the faults of others. Do not be fearful or anxious. Be of good will and without prejudice. Concentrate on the Dharma when distracted by wrong things.

'Be humble, and, if you are defeated, accept it gracefully. Give up boastfulness; renounce desire. Always generate the compassionate mind. Whatever you do, do in moderation. Be easily pleased and easily sustained. Run like a wild animal from whatever would entrap you.

'If you do not renounce worldly existence, do not say you are holy. If you have not renounced land and agriculture, do not say you have entered the sangha. If you do not renounce desire, do not say you are a monk. If you are without love and compassion, do not say you are a bodhisattva. If you do not renounce activity, do not say you are a great meditator. Do not cherish your desires.

'In short, when you stay at a monastery, engage in few activities and just meditate on the Dharma. Do not have cause for repentance at the time of death.'

At another time, Atisha stated, 'This Kaliyuga is not the time to display your ability; it is the time to persevere through hardship. It is not the time to take a high position, but the time to be humble. It is not the time to rely on many attendants, but the time to rely on isolation. Nor is it the time to subdue disciples; it is the time to subdue yourself. It is not the time of merely listening to words, but the time of contemplation on their meaning. Nor is it the time to go visiting here and there; it is the time to stay alone.'

2 *Advice from Drom*

When Atisha passed into parinirvana the teacher Drom became his successor. On one occasion his three disciples, the brothers Potowa, Chennawa and Puchungwa, asked Geshe Drom, 'Please tell us the method of practice which includes the essence of all the paths to omniscient buddhahood.'

Geshe Drom answered, 'Although there are an inconceivable number of precepts, each of which is an entrance to the path of enlightenment, there is, for one who has the necessary foundation for practice, only one thing to be obtained.'

'What is that one thing?' the three brothers asked.

'Possession of the essence of voidness and compassion. Let me explain this: voidness is the absolute bodhi-mind; it is the realization that all phenomena are by nature without truly existent birth. Compassion is the relative bodhi-mind; it is great compassion extended to all living beings who have not yet realized this fundamental birthlessness.

'Therefore, those who practise the Mahayana path should first make an effort in the method of generating these two aspects of bodhi-mind. Once this bodhi-mind has been attained, it should be diligently practised. By doing this, one is certain to manifest the rupakaya and the dharmakaya, the final effects of achieving both aspects of bodhi-mind.

'There are many methods of generating the two aspects of bodhi-mind, but condensed into a way of practice, there are no more than three root methods, and sprouting from these, nine principal branch methods. The three root methods are mind-practice, the accumulation of merit and wisdom, and the search for samadhi. Each root method has three principal branch methods.

'The three principal branch methods of mind-practice are the meditation on impermanence, the meditation on love and compassion, and the meditation on the egolessness of all persons and phenomena. Of all the various methods of mind-practice, these three are the only important ones; all others are included within them.

'The principal branch methods for the accumulation of merit and wisdom are to honour the Lama, to worship the Three Jewels and to honour the priesthood. All other methods of accumulating merit and wisdom are contained in these three; thus they are the only important ones.

'The principal methods of seeking samadhi are to maintain perfect moral practice, to pray to the Lamas of the lineage, and to maintain continual solitude. These three methods are the only important ones in seeking the highest samadhi of abiding tranquillity and intense insight; all others are included within them.

'By practising these nine methods, you will naturally produce the two aspects of bodhi-mind. When you produce the absolute bodhi-mind, you will spontaneously realize that all phenomena, whether inner or outer, are empty of real existence, from the beginning without truly existent birth, and totally free from ego-reflection. In this realization, you will find boundless joy. When you produce the relative bodhi-mind, you will generate a deep love and compassion towards all those living beings who have not realized absolute bodhi-mind. Then, whatever you do will be for nothing other than the benefit of these myriad beings, and, because you have achieved bodhi-mind, whatever you have done previously will be for their benefit also.

'There are two aspects to the conjoining of absolute and relative bodhi-mind. At the time you generate absolute bodhi-mind, you perceive the voidness of all existence. You must at this same moment of perceiving voidness generate special compassion towards all living beings, who are not negated by your perception of voidness. At the time of generating relative bodhi-mind, deep compassion towards all living beings, you must also see the non-differentiation of self and others.

'Appearances are like a magician's illusions: they are actually empty of self-nature. When you have successfully generated this unified realization of the two aspects of bodhi-mind, you have correctly entered the Mahayana path. By practising that realization, you will come to the completion of meditation and will naturally obtain the rupakaya and the dharmakaya. The dharmakaya arises from voidness – the absolute bodhi-mind; the rupakaya arises from compasssion – the relative bodhi-mind. From the inseparable practice of the two aspects of bodhi-mind, you will obtain the inseparable dharmakaya and rupakaya.'

Again the three brothers questioned their teacher Drom: 'In order to work perfectly for oneself and others, which is important, wisdom or deeds?

Drom replied, 'The person who has obtained the necessary foundation for practice and has entered the gate of the Mahayana must unify pure wisdom and pure deeds so that they may do perfect work for themself and others. Wisdom alone or deeds alone are not enough.'

'What, then, is pure wisdom, and what are pure deeds?'

'Pure wisdom consists in the realization that all existents are fundamentally free from the two extremes – eternalism, the extreme of existence, and nihilism, the extreme of non-existence. All phenomena have no *actual* existence; whether appearing inside or outside, their existence is merely relative. They are like dreams, illusions and apparitions. Furthermore, pure wisdom is the understanding that all things are but a projection of your own mind. Understanding this, you do not seek out or have attachment to anything.

'Pure deeds are understanding the infallible effects of good and bad actions in this relative existence, which is illusory and dreamlike. Further, they are striving with deep compassion, while being careful of the cause and effect of karma, for the benefit of all living beings who do not understand the nature of existence.

'Those who produce in themselves the two aspects of bodhi-mind will naturally produce pure wisdom and pure deeds.'

The disciples then asked, 'Is it wrong to have pure wisdom alone or pure deeds alone?'

Geshe Drom replied, 'If you have pure wisdom but do not have pure deeds and lose yourself in impetuous behaviour, not being careful of the cause and effect of karma, you will be of no benefit to yourself and others, and even your pure wisdom will go wrong. Should you have pure deeds but lack the perception of the fundamental voidness of all things, you will not be able to benefit yourself and others and your pure deeds will begin to go wrong. If you do not unify pure wisdom and pure deeds, you will inevitably fall into mistaken paths. Therefore, you must learn both.'

On another occasion the three brothers asked Drom, 'Which is more important, to help living beings by means of the teaching, or to practise in an isolated place?'

The teacher answered, 'Beginners who have no internal realization cannot help living beings with the teaching. Their blessing is like pouring from an empty jar – nothing will come out. Their advice is like unfermented beer – it has no essence.

'Those of admirable deeds who have not yet obtained the firmness of warmth do not have the ability to act for the benefit of living beings. Their blessing is like pouring from a full vessel – when it has filled another, it itself is empty. Their advice is like a butter lamp held in the hand: it may illuminate others, but the holder remains in the shadows.

'However, when they have entered the stages of the aryas, whatever they do brings benefit to living beings. Their blessing is like a magic vessel – though it fills countless vessels, it does not empty itself. Their advice is like a butter lamp held by the base – it illuminates others and the one who holds it as well.

'Therefore, this Kaliyuga is not the time for individuals to be of help to living beings unless they have cultivated love, compassion and bodhi-mind in isolation. It is the time to guard against fettering passions. It is not the time to cut down the seedling of the magical medicine tree, but the time to cultivate it.'

One day an old gentleman was walking round the Radreng monastery. Geshe Drom said to him, 'Sir, I am happy to see you walking round, but wouldn't you rather be practising the Dharma?'

Thinking this over, the old gentleman felt it might be better to read Mahayana sutras. While he was reading in the temple courtyard, Geshe Drom said, 'I am happy to see you reciting sutras, but wouldn't you rather be practising Dharma?'

At this, the old gentleman thought that perhaps he should meditate. He sat crosslegged on a cushion, with his eyes half closed. Drom said again, 'I am so happy to see you meditating, but wouldn't it be better to practise the Dharma?'

Now totally confused, the old gentleman asked, 'Geshe-la, please tell me what I should do to practise the Dharma.'

Drom replied, 'Renounce attraction to this life. Renounce it now. For if you do not renounce attraction to this life, whatever you do will not be the practice of the Dharma, as you have not passed beyond the eight worldly concerns. Once you have renounced this life's habitual thoughts and are no longer distracted by the eight worldly concerns, whatever you do will advance you on the path of liberation.'

'What is the difference between Dharma and non-Dharma?' the teacher Drom was asked by Potowa.

'If something is in opposition to fettering passions, it is Dharma. If it is not, it is not Dharma. If it does not accord with worldly people, it is Dharma. If it does accord, it is not Dharma. If it accords with the teachings of Buddha, it is Dharma. If it does not accord, it is not Dharma. If good follows, it is Dharma. If bad follows, it is not Dharma.'

3   Advice from other Kadampa Masters

Geshe Gonpapa said, 'Omniscience is founded on merit and wisdom. Merit and wisdom are founded on bodhi-mind. Bodhi-mind is founded on love and compassion. The precepts of all these are founded on the six transcendences.

'Further, giving is founded on non-attachment. Moral practice is founded on reliance on spiritual friends. Patience is founded on humility. Effort is founded on meditation on death. Meditation is founded on dwelling in isolation. Wisdom is founded on mindfulness. Blessings are founded on your faith and respect for the Lama and the Three Jewels. Siddhis are founded on vows and obligations. Excellence is founded on hearing, thinking and meditating. Being of service to others is founded on desirelessness. The progress of self and others is founded on meditation and devotion.'

Yerbay Shangtsun said, 'When we desire liberation from the depths of our hearts, we should, through continuous contemplation of the imminence of death, always abide in thoughts and deeds in the four qualities of the aryas.

'These four qualities of the aryas are: to be satisfied with simple religious dress, to be satisfied with meager food, to be satisfied with a poor cushion, and to be satisfied with the minimum of medicine.

'Put another way, these four are: to be desireless, to be content, to be easily sustained, and to be easily satisfied. To be desireless is to be unattached to all possessions and not to desire many or good things to maintain oneself. Contentment is to be happy with simple things. To be easily sustained means to subsist with meager and poor food, a poor cushion, and simple dress. To be easily satisfied means to be content with scant alms and recognition.

'A person who lives in this way is said to be abiding in the four qualities of the aryas, as all his practice of Dharma is directed towards enlightenment. A person who is completely taken up with worldly desires is not abiding in the four qualities of the aryas. Instead he is said to be abiding in the qualities of the devil, for abiding in non-virtuous activities is the cause of rebirth in samsara's lower states.

'If we do not give up the desires of this life now, we will come under the influence of attachment again in future lifetimes. To give up the desires of this life, the most potent countermeasure is continual meditation on impermanence. If you do not meditate on impermanence in the early morning, by midday you will have many desires.'

Geshe Potowa was asked by an upasaka. 'To actually practise the Dharma, what is most important?'

'The most important thing is the meditation on impermanence. Meditate on impermanence, the imminence of death; it will cause you to begin practising the Dharma. This will create conditions impelling you to do virtuous work, which will then assist you in realizing the equality of all things in their nature of existence.

'Meditation on impermanence will also cause you to decide to renounce the enjoyments of this life, which will create the conditions for ridding yourself of all worldly desires, and thus assist you to enter the path of nirvana.

'When you have meditated on impermanence and have gained some understanding, you will seek the Dharma. This will create the conditions for the achievement of Dharma and thus assist in its final accomplishment.

'Meditating on impermanence and finding some understanding of it will also cause you to begin to arm yourself, which will create the conditions for beginning religious practice. This will assist you in initiating the stage of non-returning.'

Geshe Chennawa, while speaking to a gathering of his disciples, said: 'In brief, the Dharma can be divided into abandoning harmful activities and taking up helpful ones. All the teachings of the higher and lower vehicles as well as the teachings of the Three Baskets are included within this precept.

'To apply this precept, patience is most important. If you are without patience and someone harms you, you will feel vengeful. Should you act on that feeling, you will not cease from harmful activities, much less be helpful to others. Therefore, patience is necessary to begin religious practice.

'To meditate on patience, there are four methods: setting up the target for the arrow; love and compassion; teacher and disciple; and meditation on the nature of existence.

'First comes meditation on the setting up of a target for the arrow: if you have not set up a target, it cannot be hit by an arrow. The arrow of harm strikes in this life because we have set up a target by the bad karma we acccumulated in previous lives. Thus it is not right to be angry with those who harm us. As Shantideva said in the *Bodhicaryavatara*:

> If I had not done harm to others,
> No harm would come to me;
> I did harm living beings –
> It is fit that harm returns to me.

Furthermore, if you have harmed others in the early part of

your life you will receive retribution in the later part of the same life. The harm done in the early part of the year will return in the later part. The same for the early and later parts of months and days. If you set up a target of bad activities and hateful speech, it will be struck by arrows of retribution. We set up the target ourselves; understand that the arrows come from our own harmful acts and do not be angry with others.

'Next comes the meditation on love and compassion. When a lunatic harms a sane person, the sane person should not return the harm by fighting him, but should say, "How sad!" The person who harms you is also insane, possessed by the madness of powerful fettering passions. Think, "How sad!" and meditate on compassion for him.

'Actually, lunatics are less crazy than the sane person who harms you, for they harm only the bodies of themselves and others and thus their harm is not so great. They are only crazy for a while, a few days, months, or years, and so the duration of their harm is not so great. Sane people who do harm, harm all sentient beings, and so they are the crazier. They come under the influence of fettering passions, which extend in the limitless world from beginningless time, and so the harm is of long duration. By carelessly committing non-virtuous deeds in body, speech and mind, they produce the misery of the three lower states. Thus their harm is very great. As they have the greater need for compassion, meditate upon love and compassion for them, and do not be angry. As Shantideva said in the *Bodhicaryavatara:*

> If one who is influenced by the fettering passions
> Will even kill himself,
> How can it be
> That he will not harm others?
> Influenced by the fettering passions
> He will destroy himself and others, too.
> If I am angry and have no compassion,
> I am worse than he.

'The third meditation on patience is on teacher and disciple. If there is no Lama to impart instruction, there can be no vow. If there is no teacher to explain the Dharma, there can be no realization. Similarly, if there is no enemy who harms you, there can be no practice of patience; therefore you should feel that those who abuse you are the teachers of patience. Be happy at this opportunity and concentrate on repaying their kindness. Meditating that you are a disciple being taught patience, do not be angry.

'To meditate on the nature of existence as voidness, contemplate that all three aspects of harmfulness – the agent of harm, the recipient of harm, and the act of harming – are all void of self-nature. As all these things which you now see opposing you are erroneous creations of your mind, like dreams and illusions, it is not right to be angry. As Shantideva said in the *Bodhicaryavatara*:

> From being praised,
> What do you gain, what do you lose?
> In being despised,
> Why be happy, why be sad?

When you wake from sleep, you understand that the enemies in your dreams have no self-nature and you are not angry with them. As your actual enemy is also without self-nature, do not be angry with him, and meditate on patience.'

Geshe Chennawa said, 'In order to obtain omniscience and liberation we must learn not to conform with worldly people. Such people value Buddha more than living beings, value self more than others, value those who are helpful more than those who are harmful, and value happiness more than misery.

'Those who practise Dharma must do the opposite. We should value living beings more than Buddha. Why is this? Not only is it not disrespectful to value living beings more than Buddha, but there are four good reasons for doing so:

all living beings in samsara are our kind mothers; as these mothers suffer in samsara, we must help them; by helping them we will naturally achieve our own purpose; and by helping them we respect and worship all the Buddhas and bodhisattvas.

'Worldly people value themselves more than others, but we must value others more than ourselves. Why? From beginningless time we have created our own misery; it has not been created by others. Misery is brought about by our own fettering passions. As egoism and fettering passions are one, it is our own egoism which has created our misery. Therefore, we must oppose this enemy in every way, and value others more than ourselves, since it is in relation to other living beings that we accumulate merit and wisdom. Also, it is in relation to other living beings that we meditate on the two aspects of bodhi-mind which lead to the attainment of nirvana.

'Worldly people value those who help them more than those who harm them; we must do the opposite. Why is this? In this world, parents are considered to be the greatest help, for they give their children servants, wives and husbands, herds of horses, palaces, gold, turquoise, and land. Yet, according to the Dharma, there is no greater harm that that, because, desiring these gifts, children accumulate and extend bad karma and fettering passions, and by this they may finally fall into hell. What appears now to be help has an end result of misery, and the kind fathers and mothers of this life can thus be considered our greatest enemies. We must instead value those who bring us harm. Why? When harmed by an enemy, we can meditate on patience, and from patience we obtain immeasurable merit. When harmed by devils we begin to make an effort, and, travelling higher and higher paths, we obtain all siddhis. Thus we must value those who harm us.

'Finally, worldly people value happiness more than misery; we must do the opposite. Why is this? Desire for the happiness of food and clothes, of idleness, of sex, of rest, and of sleep is finally the cause of despair. Therefore we must value misery more than worldly happiness. Why is this? By the misery of work undertaken for the Lama and the priesthood, by the misery of the hardships of moral practice, and by the misery undergone while doing virtuous work in body, speech and mind, we purify defilements and accomplish merit and wisdom. By these we obtain states of great spiritual happiness; therefore we must value misery. When troubled in mind and sick in body, we can turn from samsara and produce the mind of renunciation. Therefore we must value misery.'

Geshe Chennawa said, 'Nowadays even the best people mix their religious practice with worldly interests. Afraid of weakness, they seek patronage with families of great name. Afraid of devils, they recite mantras of the wrathful deities. Afraid of starvation, they accumulate many possessions. Afraid of being criticized, they act hypocritically.

'Among such people do you think any will become Buddha? It isn't likely. Do you think a sheep can rise up when the butcher is grasping him for slaughter? Do you think he can free himself when he is already butchered? It isn't likely.

'What should be done? If someone harms you, do not retaliate, but meditate on patience. If you do that, you will not be overcome by even the most powerful person. Therefore, as the chief strength is meditation on patience, it is senseless to seek patronage.

'If devils come, seeking to trouble you, realize that, like the horns of a hare, an independent ego does not exist; if you give up life and body to the devils, even the demons of the three thousand worlds cannot harm you. Therefore, the principal power is the realization of egolessness, and it is senseless to recite mantras of wrathful deities.

'If you are completely impoverished, you will entrust yourself to Dharma. As a final consequence of turning towards the Dharma, you will entrust yourself to the life of a beggar. As a final consequence of this, you will entrust yourself to death. Because of your holy life, after your death you will be revered by all those faithful to the Teaching. Therefore, the greatest joy is found in non-attachment and it is meaningless to accumulate possessions.

'If you are without hypocrisy, although some may criticize you, you will actually be most admirable. Therefore, as the basis of a good name is to be without falsehood in thought or deed, it is useless to act hypocritically.'

Geshe Puchungwa said: 'Though we have obtained the indispensable human body with its leisure and opportunity, we do not have the power to stay in it – we have to die. At the time of death, we cannot take with us any of the enjoyments or concepts of this life, just as a tree sheds all its leaves. At that time the measure of our knowledge, our strength, and the wisdom of our goals will be clear. When we face death happily and with joyful anticipation, we are wise and strong; our goals are noble, and we will enter death clearheaded. But if at that time the form of Yama and the distinct sign of lower states of birth appear, our goals were foolish and we are without self-mastery.

'We, for the most part, follow the wrong path, seeking to fulfil the desires of this life. The perfect Buddha never spoke falsely. The authors of the commentaries, such as Nagarjuna, never spoke falsely. The holy spiritual friends do not speak falsely. Then how do we enter the wrong path? By the desires of this life. Thus we should always contemplate death, for remembering the imminence of death we understand the need for non-attachment to this life. We should contemplate the perniciousness of all samsara, for then we understand the need to be unattached to the whole of it. By remembering living beings in the meditation on love, compassion and bodhi-mind, we understand the need to be unattached to our selfish goals. By remembering egolessness in the meditation on the voidness of all things, we understand the need to be unattached to objects and attributes.'

Again Geshe Puchungwa said, 'To practise Dharma earnestly, you must be like a small bird. As a sparrow is unable to mingle with hawks, you should not mingle with worldly people, for if you do so you will be carried away by devils. When worldly people dislike you, it is just what you want, for then they will leave you alone. Because of their insults, others will leave you alone. Also, although you have nothing but an ounce of barley flour, if your mind is tranquil and happy, you can do virtuous work. If you increase your virtuous work, you will increase your knowledge and by that you will naturally benefit living beings.'

Geshe Nyugrumpa said, 'You who wish to obtain rebirth as a human being or god, and also wish to obtain perfect enlightenment, must think of samsara as a prison. You should see this life and body as a bubble of water, bad company as an enemy, the spiritual teacher as a wish-fulfilling jewel, the fettering passions as a poisonous snake, sinful activities as strong poison, the aspects of desire as the embers of a fire, sweet words and fame as an echo, respect and gain as an entangling snare, bad friends as a contagious disease, good friends as a beautiful and fortified palace, all sentient beings as your mother and father. You should feel that giving is the wish-fulfilling cow, that moral practice is a precious jewelled ornament, that patience is strong armour, that effort is the wish-fulfilling wisdom-horse, that meditation is a great treasure, and that the wisdom of hearing, thinking and meditation is a bright lamp.'

Geshe Kharawa said, 'As a person who has no faith has no

chance of developing excellence you should rely on the spiritual teacher and read the sutras. As a person who makes no effort has no chance of developing excellence, you should meditate on impermanence, and abandon laziness. As a person who has pride has no chance of developing excellence, you should be self-effacing and humble. If you do these things, you have the right basis for becoming a sravaka, a bodhisattva, or a practitioner of the Mantrayana – in short, you have the proper basis for all excellence.'

Again, Geshe Kharawa said, 'It is a mistake not to see that attachment is harmful, for it keeps us from rising from samsara. It is a mistake not to see that anger is harmful, for anger destroys the root of virtue. It is a mistake not to see that pride is harmful, for pride stunts the root of virtue, preventing the growth of excellence.

'Do not despise giving; by giving we obtain the spiritual pleasures of humans and gods. Do not despise moral practice; by moral practice we obtain rebirth as human or god. Do not despise compassion, for it is the source of all the Mahayana teaching. Do not despise the bodhisattva precepts, for the bodhisattva vow is the special method of achieving perfect omniscience. Do not despise the Mantrayana vow, for through the Mantrayana you can quickly obtain the ordinary and higher siddhis.'

He also said, 'The culmination of wisdom is freedom from all assertions. The culmination of meditation is freedom from all mental activities. The culmination of deeds is freedom from all discrimination. The culmination of practice is freedom from all superfluous experience.'

Geshe Naysurpa said, 'As you will not reach Buddhahood by conceiving of others as your adversaries, you must realize that all livings beings are your mother and father. As you will not obtain Buddhahood by the habitual concepts of the ordinary mind, you must realize that all sentient beings are deities. As you will not obtain Buddhahood by distinguishing attributes, you must realize that voidness is the nature of all living beings.'

Geshe Langritangpa said, 'As one person cannot truly take the measure of another, do not criticize anyone. As all the Buddha's teachings are effective, do not discriminate between them, saying that some are good and some bad. As all the deeds of the Mahayana are for the benefit of all beings, do not weaken the armour of the bodhisattva path. As you cannot lead others until you have achieved stability yourself, make effort and meditate in isolation.'

Geshe Chayulpa said, 'Object and subject are like sandalwood and its fragrance. Samsara and nirvana are like ice and water. Appearances and voidness are like clouds and sky. Voidness and habitual thoughts are like the ocean and its waves.'

Geshe Tolungpa said, 'If you desire liberation from the depths of your heart, you must follow the holy rather than the clever teacher. You must follow those who devote themselves to the teaching rather than those who explain it, those who are humble rather than those who have great position, those of faith rather than those famous for their intelligence. There is no harm if you do not know the teaching, but misfortune will come if you follow those whose actions are contrary to the Dharma.'

Geshe Shabogaypa also said, 'As the desires of this life cause all the misery of this and future lives, we must not seek the fulfilment of our desires. When we try to fulfil our desires, we are not happy. We become unsure of the direction of our life, and wrong speech, wrong mind and wrong actions all surface at once.

'Therefore we must turn away from our many desires. When we are able to do this, we establish the beginnings of happiness and pleasure. The best sign of happiness in this and all future lives is not desiring or accumulating anything at all. When we do not desire gain, we have the greatest gain. When we do not desire reputation, we have the best reputation. When we do not desire fame, we have the greatest fame. When we do not desire companions, we have the best companions.

'If we are to sincerely practise the Dharma, we must entrust ourselves wholeheartedly to the life of a mendicant, for mendicants are those who entrust themselves to death. When we can produce this feeling, neither gods, nor devils can conquer us. But when we indulge in the desires of this life, we lower ourselves and make ourselves completely miserable. We bring censure on ourselves in this life and rebirth in lower states in future lives.

'Therefore, when, not wishing our own happiness, we limit our criticism of others, humble ourselves, limit our desires, and avoid all activities that are not religious, we will then obtain enlightenment in the future.

'In short, we are always beginning what is not necessary to begin, realizing what is not necessary to realize, doing what is not necessary to do. Though we say all this, if we do not actually turn away from the desires of this life, there is no way of seeking happiness now or in future lives. If we turn away from all desires, we do not need to seek happiness at all.'

Finally, Geshe Shabogaypa chastised himself: 'You old fool – you wish for high teachings, though your nature is low. You charlatan – you desire to improve others, but do not improve yourself. You sham – you act as if Dharma were meant only for others to follow, and not for yourself. You blunderer – you have charged others to act correctly, but act incorrectly yourself. You shiftless bum – each rise precedes a greater fall. You politician – you make extensive promises but abbreviated application. You rascal – you seek fettering passions, and at the same time pretend to apply their countermeasures. You coward – you are fearful of others seeing your faults and hope that they will see only your good qualities.

'You involve yourself with your relatives instead of cultivating spiritual friends. You involve yourself with fettering passions instead of cultivating their antidotes. You leave practice for future lives instead of cultivating it in this life. You involve yourself with those who help you rather than cultivating those who harm you.

'You idiot – you harm others, not knowing you harm yourself. You do not know that to help others is to help yourself. You do not see that misery and harm which come to you are conducive to practising Dharma. You do not see that desire and happiness are not conducive to the practice of Dharma.

'You say to others that practising Dharma is very important, yet do not follow the teaching yourself. You despise others who are sinful, yet do not stop your own wrongdoing. You see the slightest faults in others, yet do not perceive great faults in yourself. You soon stop helping others when you get nothing in return. You cannot bear to see other teachers receive respect. You are subservient to those in high positions while contemptuous of those beneath you. Talk of future lives is not pleasing to your ears. You act holy and disdainful when corrected by others. You want others to see your virtues and are content when they do not see your faults. You are satisfied with a good façade while what is inside is not so good.

'You like to be given things. Not seeking happiness within yourself, you seek it externally. Having vowed to learn Buddha's teaching, you learn worldly affairs instead.

Though you agree with the advice of the bodhisattvas, your actions are preparing you for hell. Though you have dedicated your body, enjoyment, and virtuous activities of past, present and future for the benefit of all living beings, you refuse to give up your ego. You like sinful friends, forgetting that they lead to ruin. You do not know that the anger of a spiritual friend is helpful.

'Do not waste time in pointless debate. Do not build castles in the air, increasing your cravings. Do not delight in dangerous activities. Do not do those many things which senselessly hinder virtuous work.'

Feeling self-reproach, he scolded himself in this way.

This is the lineage of Atisha's teaching, the heartfelt speech of many holy beings. These precepts were collected in different places by the venerable Tsunbajegom.

Part Three
The Kagyu Tradition

The Songs of Jetsun Milarepa

Look up into the sky,
And practise meditation free from the fringe and centre.
Look up at the sun and moon,
And practise meditation free from bright and dim.
Look over at the mountains,
And practise meditation free from departing and changing.
Look down at the lake,
And practise meditation free from waves.
Look here at your mind,
And practise meditation free from discursive thought.

Milarepa

Introduction to Part Three

Milarepa is undoubtedly one of the most popular and highly esteemed teachers in the history of Tibetan Buddhism. Although he was one of the founding figures of the Kagyu tradition, he is held in veneration by all the schools. When young, he studied black magic in order to avenge himself on some relatives who had maltreated him and his mother. As a consequence of these studies he was able to kill several people by sorcery. Afterwards he regretted what he had done and went to the teacher Marpa to receive instruction in Buddhism. First, Marpa made him undergo many trials and hardships in order to purify his mind of the negative karma of killing. He finally received initiation into the practices of the Vajrayana and devoted the remainder of his life to meditation and teaching, often in remote mountainous regions.

Milarepa usually expressed his understanding in the form of songs. After his death these, together with stories about his life, were recorded by his disciples. Here are just three of the many songs attributed to him. The first, *The Virtues of the Realization of Bliss and Warmth*, gives a moving account of the joy and fortitude that sustained Milarepa during his years of austerity. In the second, *Red Rock Agate Mansion*, the quality of profound devotion to one's spiritual master that is required to realize the goal of the Vajrayana is shown through Milarepa's heartfelt recollection and subsequent vision of his teacher Marpa. The final section, *At the Kungthang Fair*, tells of his meeting with Paldarbum and the series of instructions he gave her on the practice of Buddhism.

These songs were translated into English by the Nalanda Translation Committee under the direction of the Vajracarya Chögyam Trungpa Rinpoche as part of *The Rain of Wisdom*, a classical anthology of the songs and teachings of the lamas in the Kagyu tradition. This text first appeared in English in 1980.

1 *The Virtues of the Realization of Bliss and Warmth*

Mila's sister asked, 'Singing songs by day and sleeping at night, hasn't your mind become distracted?'

Mila thought. 'She is right,' and held more firmly to his body, speech and mind. He did not take the time to fix up the clothing given him by his sister. He tightened up the three points: the upright posture, the point of body; the seal-knot, the point of speech; and the snake-knot, the point of mind. Whether dead or not, whether collapsed or not, he practised. In eighteen days, bliss and warmth blazed up spontaneously. The clothing given him by his sister was eaten by insects and mildew, and fell to pieces.

One day his sister returned and asked. 'Did you fix up the clothing?'

Mila replied, 'I didn't fix up the clothing; the insects ate it.'

She said, 'You have wasted the cloth! Now aren't you embarrassed to be naked?'

So Mila sang his song:

> I supplicate the lord gurus.
> Grant your blessings so that this lowly one may keep to retreat.

Sister, you make embarrassing what is not embarras-
  sing.
The boy on one's lap comes from an embarrassing act.
The bride that one buys is likewise embarrassing.
One ages and still commits embarrassing acts.
This here is the natural mark of a male.
After one has been given the name of a man or a
  woman,
Everybody knows that you have this here.

You do not shrink from what is truly embarrassing or
  indecent.
Evil actions, deceit, stealing.
Bad deeds, evil dispositions, perverted views.
Selling one's friends and relatives
Are embarrassing and indecent actions but no one
  shrinks from them.
The secret actions of the profound vajra
And all the great meditators of the profound oral
  instructions
Who bring dharma to one's life
Have no fear of embarrassment for even one moment.

Petama, don't be sad and petty-minded.
Don't stay depressed; go and beg.

With a great effort, Mila practised and practised. But as
nettles alone were not sufficient as food, his practice grew
weaker and weaker, and his faculties became feeble.
  One day, some hunters carrying the meat of a deer they
had killed came near the rocks where Mila was living. They
became curious and called many times. When the jetsun
finally looked at them, they asked. 'Are you Mila
Thöpaga?'
  He answered, 'I am.'
  They said, 'You have dwelt among these rocks. What
virtues do these rocks have?'
  In answer, Mila sang this song:

The blessings of the lord guru have entered these
    rocks.
If you do not know the virtues of these rocks,
This is the Lofty Green Mountain Sky Fortress.

At the palace of the Sky Fortress,
Above, dark clouds gather;
Below, blue rivers flow;
Behind, the red rock sky fortress.
In front, the meadows are beautiful with flowers.
On the border, beasts of prey cry out.
To the side, the king of birds, the vulture soars.
At times, a gentle rain falls.
Constantly, the bees hum a melodious song.
The deer and wild horses, mothers and young, play
    and frolic.
The songbirds, mothers and young, sing many
    beautiful songs.
The divine bird, the white grouse, sings a melodious
    song.
Springs trickle from the rocks and make a pleasant
    sound.
The different sounds of the four seasons are friends of
    the mind.
The virtues of this place are inconceivable.

I have sung this song of joy,
I have uttered these oral instructions,
And I have explained them to you hunters.
Do not commit evil deeds! Be virtuous!

The hunters said that his song was truly wonderful, and
offered him their venison and their remaining tsampa (barley flour). After Mila had cooked and eaten the meat, his
body felt comfortable and his meditation became very
strong. Since his body felt healthy and well and his mind
was clear, his practice became excellent.

In a day or two, an old hunter returned, bringing Mila some tsampa. He asked Mila, 'How is your health now?'

Mila replied, 'I am well,' and sang this song:

> In the White Rock Lofty Meadow Palace
> Milarepa's meditation goes well.
> Without fixation or attachment, both moving and
>   staying go well.
> Free from sickness, my body is well.
> Not falling asleep, my posture goes well.
> Not thinking, my samadhi goes well.
> Not getting cold, my candali goes well.
> Undiminished, my yogic discipline goes well.
> Not making an effort, my harvesting goes well.
> Not being distracted, my solitude goes well.
> These are the ways of conducting my body.
>
> The vehicle of skilful means and knowledge goes well.
> The practice of the unity of utpatti and sampanna-
>   krama goes well.
> Prana being free from coming and going, my mind is
>   well.
> Without friends to converse with, giving up conversa-
>   tion goes well.
> These are the ways of conducting my speech.
>
> Free from grasping, the view goes well.
> Without interruption, meditation goes well.
> Without being reticent, action goes well.
> Without hope and fear, the fruition goes well.
> These are the ways of conducting my mind.
>
> Unchanging and without thought, luminosity goes
>   well.
> In the realm of pure great bliss, I am well.
> In space open to unobstructed arising, I am well.
> This is a little song of complete well-being.
>
> Having sung this song of experience,
> The oral instructions have escaped from my mouth.

Here, view and action are united.
Henceforth, for those who wish to attain enlighten-
ment,
If you practise, practise like this.

The patron rejoined, prostrated many times, and went
home.

In a day or two, the patron, accompanied by some
friends, each bringing some tsampa, returned. They said,
'Guru, sir, the song you sang the other day was very good.
But having very little knowledge, we did not understand it.
Please teach us that clear meaning in a few words.'

So Mila sang this song.

The blessings of the lord guru have entered these
rocks.
Grant your blessings so that this lowly one may
remain among these rocks.

Faith, learning and discipline,
These three are the life-tree of the mind.
When it is planted and planted firmly, all goes well.
If you plant a life-tree, plant it like this.
Non-desire, non-attachment, non-delusion,
These three are the armour of the mind.
When worn, it is light and impregnable.
If you wear armour, wear it like this.

Meditation, exertion and endurance,
These three are the stallion of the mind.
When it runs, it is fast; when in flees, it escapes.
If you ride a stallion, ride it like this.

Self-existing insight, luminosity and bliss,
These three are the fruit of the mind.
When it is planted, it ripens; when it is eaten, it
nourishes.
If you grow fruit, grow it like this.

These twelve meanings of the mind

> Have dawned in the mind of this yogin, and so I sing of
>   them.
> Take these responses, faithful patron.

Thus, Mila sang.

Then the faithful patron known as Shen Dormo said,
'Please say it still more concisely, condensed into one
word.'
So Mila sang this song:

> The blessings of the guru have entered my mind.
> Grant your blessings so that I may realize my mind as
>   shunyata.
>
> This is my gift to the faithful benefactor.
> I will sing a song to please the divine yidams.
>
> Appearance and emptiness and their inseparability,
> These three are the synopsis of the view.
>
> Luminosity, non–thought, and non–
>   wandering,
> These three are the synopsis of meditation.
>
> Non–attachment, non–desire and non–
>   confusion.
> These three are the synopsis of action.
> No hope, no fear, and no completion,
> These three are the synopsis of fruition.
>
> Free in public, free in private, not deceiving,
> These three are the synopsis of samaya.

Thus, Mila sang.

The benefactor was delighted and went home. In general,
the people of Nyenam had faith, but few resources. Thus,
they were not able to offer Mila very much and so his
spiritual practice was not stolen away by charity. Milarepa
said, 'As I did have weak soup for five or six months, I was
not blown away by the wind of starvation.'
These were the songs of Lofty Green Mountain.

2 Red Rock Agate Mansion

Having spent six years at Lofty Green Mountain, Mila went to the Red Rock Agate Mansion Fortress of Garudas. He thought, 'May I die while fulfilling my vow to practise for twelve years, twelve months, twelve days and twelve hours – four sets of twelve. May I die meditating, without the people of the land knowing where I am.'

Death never came, but Mila's health deteriorated, and he thought, 'I have already given up worldly activities. Since I have not died yet, I shall do nothing but practise the Dharma. Therefore, I must cook and eat some nettles.' He then went to gather some wood. He found some twigs and put them on top of a flat rock. While he rested, a wind arose and scattered the wood. 'All is impermanent like this: when will impermanence catch up with me?' wondered Mila. 'Still, I have to gather wood.' As he broke off a large dry branch, he fell down in a faint.

A cold gusty wind whistled at dusk as the sun set. When Mila awoke and came to his senses, he was overcome by a sad and intense depression. He looked to the east, in the direction of the guru's residence. There he saw a floating white cloud and he remembered his guru with longing. He sang this song of the six remembrances of the guru:

I supplicate the lord gurus.
Accept me with kindness and make this lowly one's
    depression vanish.

Beneath this cloud that floats above in the east,
At the monastery in Trowo Valley of the south
Dwells my guru.
If one utters his name, it is Marpa the translator.
What joy if he were there now.
What happiness if he were there now.
Although he is far away, I long to see him.
Although it is a hard journey, I long to see him.
Sho mo! I remember the guru once again.
Thinking further, I remember the jetsun more.

Dagmema, the lady who pleases the Buddha,
What joy if she were there now.
What happiness if she were there now.
Although I have no gift for the mother, I long to see
    her.
Although I have no offerings, I long to see her.
Sho mo! I remember the guru once again.
Thinking further, I remember the jetsun more.

The four sign empowerments of the profound
    abhiseka,
What joy if they were being performed now.
What happiness if they were being performed now.
Although I have little to offer, I long to make an offer-
    ing.
Although my provisions are few, I long to receive
    abhiseka.
Sho mo! I remember the guru once again.
Thinking further, I remember that jetsun more.

The profound tantra of Hevajra,
What joy if it were being received now.
What happiness if it were being received now.
Although I am poor in knowledge, I long to receive it.

Although my wits are dull, I long to hear it.
Sho mo! I remember the guru once again.
Thinking further, I remember the jetsun more.

The profound instruction of the six dharmas of
    Naropa,
What joy if it were being received now.
What happiness if it were being received now.
Although my exertion in meditation is feeble, I long to
    meditate.
Although my constitution is feeble, I long to meditate.
Sho mo! I remember the guru once again.
Thinking further, I remember the jetsun more.

The gatherings of the faithful brothers from Ü and
    Tsang,
What joy if they were there now.
What happiness if they were there now.
I long to compare notes and enter the discussions.
I long to converse with them and compare experi-
    ences.
Sho mo! I remember the guru once again.
Thinking further, I remember the jetsun more.

The castle that pleases the guru,
What joy if I were building it now.
What happiness if I were building it now.
Although I am getting old, I long to build it.
Although this illusory body is deteriorating, I long to
    build it.
Sho mo! I remember the guru once again.
Thinking further, I remember the jetsun more.

My honoured parents, who are so kind,
What joy if they were there now.
What happiness if they were there now.
I long to repay my father's and mother's kindness.
I long to serve them however I can.
Sho mo! I remember the guru once again.

> Thinking further, I remember the jetsun more.
> Great Vajradhara, source of blessings,
> Grant your blessings so that this lowly one's sadness
>   may be cleared away.

Thus, Mila sang.

The cloud stretched out towards him, closer and closer, like a bolt of cloth unrolling. When it was above his head, Mila saw on the tip of it guru Marpa himself, riding an unbridled white lioness. Marpa said, 'Milarepa, what has happened that today you have made such great lamentation? Has faith in the guru arisen? Or have distracting thoughts led you to pursue the phenomenal world? Have obstacles of desiring happiness entered your practice place? Have you been irritated by the claustrophobia of ghostly thoughts of hope and fear? What happened? You and I are beyond meeting and parting.'

Mila's joy was so great that he was struck speechless and realization beyond analogy dawned. He experienced that which is beyond words and sang this song of devotion and supplication:

> Having seen the face and heard the voice of the lord
>   guru,
> This lowly one's depression turns into meditative
>   experience.

> Thinking about the guru's kindness,
> The devotion of realization arises from my depths.
> Because you bestowed your kind blessings in person,
> Non-dharmic appearances are completely cut off.

> Although this lamentation in an empty unpeopled
>   valley
> Irritates the ear of the father guru,
> This lowly one could be satisfied by nothing other
>   than the guru's appearance.

This practice of perseverance and asceticism
Is service pleasing to the father guru.

This solitary retreat free from sickness
Is service pleasing to the mother dakinis.
This ascetic life of bearing hunger and accepting
    death
Is a gift to sentient beings who have no protector.

This perseverance, alone and without friends
Is the broom which sweeps away karma and its
    ripening.

These dharma provisions of inexhaustible nettles
Are the favourable condition for the arising of
    experience and realization

The kindness of the father guru is repaid by
    practice.
Lord guru, please keep me in your kind heart.
Grant your blessings so that this lowly one may
    keep to retreat.

Thus, Mila sang.

Mila's mind became blissful and he carried some wood
back up to the cave. When he arrived there, he found in the
cave seven metal apsaras with bodies the size of thumbs and
eyes the size of cups. Some were making fire, some were
bringing water, some were grinding tsampa, and some sat
performing various magical tricks.

As soon as Mila saw them he became frightened. He
meditated on his deity, uttered a subjugating mantra, performed a gaze, and aroused the deity's presence. He then
meditated on compassion and friendliness, but was still
unable to pacify them. He thought, 'These might be the
local deities of this place. Although I have been here for
months and years, I have not praised them or given them
any *torma*.' So he sang a song of praise to that place:

E ma! This sacred ground of solitary retreat
Is the place where victorious ones have attained
   enlightenment.

This place where I dwell alone
Is the Red Rock Agate Mansion Fortress of Garudas.

Above, grey clouds gather
And the vulture sweeps and soars.

In the valley the river swirls and churns,
And fish and otters swim and dive.

Behind, the king of mountains has a lofty peak
Where various kinds of trees and shrubs blossom.

In front are hills like heaps of rice
Where springs and flowers abound.

At the foot is a marsh with dice-like spots
Where deer, wild asses, and·their young play.

Leaves and flowers are shaped like lotuses
Where blackbirds sing melodiously.

There are many rock and slate snow mountains
Where ptarmigan sing beautifully.

Between highlands and lowlands
There are no human footprints,
Which makes this sacred ground suitable for
   enlightenment.

In this sacred ground of solitary retreat,
I, Milarepa, keep to my practice;
The root of practice is bodhicitta.

You non-human demons assembled here are
   obstacles.
Drink this amrita of friendliness and compassion and
   be gone.

Thus, Mila sang.

Three apsaras who were performing magic went away, but Mila was still unable to make the other four go away. Realizing that the four demons were magical obstacles, he sang this song of confidence in the experiences and view:

> I am the scion of a white lioness.
> As a cub, I led the pride.
> As a full-grown lion, I roam the snow ranges.
> Even my enemy, the swirling snowstorm, does not intimidate me.
>
> I am the scion of a garuda, king of birds.
> As a chick, I led the flock.
> As a full-grown garuda, I soar through the heights.
> Even towering precipices do not intimidate me.
>
> I am the scion of the great fish, the salmon.
> As a young fish, I compassed the far reaches of the lake.
> As a mature fish, I roam the rivers.
> Even the rapids do not intimidate me.
> I am the scion of the great Naropa.
> As a novice meditator, I studied with my guru.
> As a mature meditator, I roam the mountain solitudes.
> You maras and obstacles do not intimidate me.
>
> It is wonderful that you demons came today.
> You must come again tomorrow.
> From time to time we should converse.

Thus, Mila sang.

Three of the apsaras vanished like a rainbow. The remaining apsara performed an imposing dance, and Mila thought, 'This one is vicious and very powerful.' So he sang this song of the view, the pinnacle of realization:

> The paws of a lion crouching in the snow are never cold.
> If the paws of a lion crouching in the snow could get cold,

The three powers of a lion would have little meaning.

The bird that soars the skies cannot fall.
If the bird that soars the skies could fall,
The broad six wings of a bird would have little
meaning.

The fish that dwells in the water cannot drown.
If the fish that dwells in the water could drown,
The round golden eye of a fish would be of little
meaning.

An iron boulder cannot be broken by stone.
If an iron boulder could be broken by stone.
Highly refined iron would have little meaning.

My realization of the nature of mind has no fear of
demons.
If my realization of the nature of mind had fear of
demons,
Living among high rocks would have little meaning.

A demon like you does not intimidate me.
If a demon like you could intimidate me,
The arising of the mind of compassion would be of
little meaning.

Demon, if you were to stay here longer, that would be
fine with me.
If you have friends, bring them along.
We will talk out our differences.
Ah tsa ma! I feel compassion for this spirit.

Lord Vajradhara, whose essence is Aksobhya,
Grant your blessings so that this lowly one may have
complete compassion.

Thus, Mila sang.

With friendliness and compassion, and without concern for his body, Mila placed himself in the mouth of the demon; but the demon could not eat him and so vanished like a rainbow.

All this is the chapter on the Red Rock Agate Mansion.

3   *At the Kungthang Fair*

The jetsun then went south towards Lhogo in Kungthang, where there were many people who had gathered for a fair. Among them was a very handsomely dressed young woman who said, 'Yogin, what is your country and who are your father, mother and relatives?'

In reply, Mila sang this song:

> I prostrate to the lord gurus.
> I ask you to grant your blessings.
>
> My father is the all-good.
> My mother is the good being.
> My elder brother is the king of learning.
> My aunt is the luminous torch.
> My sister is the lady of faith.
> My friend is the self-existing wisdom.
> My son is the little child of insight.
> My books are the natural existence of the phenomenal
>   world.
> I ride the stallion of the wind of consciousness.
> My patrons are the four provinces of Ü and Tsang.
> I myself am the little white offering attendant.

Thus, Mila sang.

The maiden said, 'A la la, how wondrous, how great indeed. But we worldly persons do not understand. Please tell us what you mean.'

So Mila sang this song:

> I never repeat a previous song.
> But now I will explain this clearly.
>
> My only father, the all-good,
> Gave me as allowance the view and meditation:
> I never had a worldly idea.
>
> My mother, the good being,
> Nursed me with the teat of oral instruction:
> I was never starved for practice.
>
> My elder brother, the king of learning,
> Gave me the sword of prajna and upaya:
> I cut the doubt about outer and inner dharmas.
> My aunt, the luminous torch,
> Made me look into the mirror of my mind;
> This has never been tarnished by the dirt of habitual
>   patterns.
>
> My sister, the lady of faith,
> Untied the knot of miserliness;
> This yogin never had food or wealth.
> Even if I had, I would never have scrimped and saved.
>
> My friend, the self-existing wisdom,
> Was my inseparable companion;
> We never had the bad tempers to fight.
>
> My son, the child of insight,
> Holds the family lineage of the victorious ones;
> I never raised a snot-nosed child.
>
> My books, the natural existence of the phenomenal
>   world,
> Reveal understanding;
> I never looked at the black letters of books.

I ride the stallion of the wind of consciousness;
Wherever I want to go, he takes me there;
I never rode a horse of flesh and blood.

The patrons, the four provinces of Ü and Tsang,
Provided me with the food I needed to live;
I never had to strangle the tsampa bag.

I myself am the little white offering attendant.
'Offering' means that I offer worship to the three
   jewels.
'Attendant' means that I attend to my guru.
'White' means the white of the Dharma.
'Little' means that my klesas are few.
This is why I am the little white offering attendant.

Thus, Mila sang.

The maiden said, 'A la la, that is excellent. When you
come among us, you must be beyond a sense of samsara.'
   The jetsun sang this song:

When I look over at samsara, the enemy,
At first samsara is a joyful experience.
Later its appearances are deceptive.
Finally it is a prison without escape.
I am nauseated by the extent of samsara.

When you look over at your lover,
First your lover is a smiling goddess,
Later she is a vicious woman.
Finally she is a black-faced demoness.
Desire for a lover is disastrous.

When you look over at your child,
First your child is a soft-spoken young god.
Later he is a distant-hearted neighbour.
Finally he is an antagonistic creditor.
It is a great mistake to feed an ungrateful enemy.

When you look over at your wealth,

First your wealth is a precious jewel.
Later you cannot get along without it.
Finally it is like bees collecting honey;
Whatever you have painfully amassed is taken by
    others.

Think on this and practise the divine Dharma.
Then at least you will not feel regret at the moment of
    death.

Thus, Mila sang.

Faith arose in the maiden and she said, 'Yogin, do you
have a good Dharma lineage?'
In reply, Mila sang this song:

Samantabhadra, the all-pervading dharmakaya,
Great Vajradhara, the sambhogakaya
    ornamented with the marks,

Shakyamuni, the nirmanakaya who benefits
    beings –
This yogin possesses these three lineages.
Do you have the good fortune to have faith
    in these three lineages?

Thus, Mila sang.

The maiden said, 'Your lineage is good, but do you have
a good guru?'
In reply, Mila sang this song:

My outer guru manifests outwardly as the wisdom
    lineage.
My inner guru manifests internally as the insight
    lineage.
My ultimate guru arises in my mind as the ultimate
    lineage.
This yogin possesses these three gurus.
Would the young lady have faith in these three gurus?

Thus, Mila sang.

The maiden said, 'You have met with such gurus, but did you receive abhiseka?'

> The outer abhiseka is placing the vase on the head.
> The inner abhiseka is the transmission showing one's body as the body of the deity.
> The ultimate abhiseka is the transmission showing the mind as bliss–emptiness.
> This yogin possesses these three abhisekas.
> Would the young lady receive these three abhisekas?

Thus, Mila sang.

The maiden said, 'You have received profound abhisekas. Afterwards, did you receive the oral instructions?'

In reply, Mila sang this song:

> The outer instruction is learning, contemplation and meditation.
> The inner instruction is insight when rock meets bone.
> The ultimate instruction is free from union or separation with experience.
> This yogin possesses these three instructions.
> Would the young lady receive these three instructions?

Thus, Mila sang.

The maiden said, 'You have received such instructions. Afterwards, did you wander in haunted grounds?'

In reply, Mila sang this song:

> The outer chöd is wandering in haunted grounds.
> The inner chöd is setting out your body as carrion.
> The ultimate chöd is to completely cut with PHAT alone.
> This yogin possesses these three chöds.
> Would the young lady practise these three chöds?

Thus, Mila sang.

The maiden said, 'As PHAT is needed in the practice of chöd, what is the meaning of PHAT?'

In reply, Mila sang this song:

The outer PHAT is gathering the scattered.
The inner PHAT clears drowsiness.
The ultimate PHAT cuts the ground and root of mind.
This yogin possesses these three rounds of PHAT.
Would the young lady practise these three rounds of
    PHAT?

Thus, Mila sang.
The maiden said, 'After having practised PHAT, what are
the ground, path and fruition like?'
In reply, Mila sang this song:

The unfabricated ground is the great all–pervading.
The unfabricated path is the great transparency.
The unfabricated fruition is mahamudra.
This yogin possesses these three: ground, path and
    fruition.
Would the young lady possess these three: ground,
    path and fruition?

Thus, Mila sang.
The maiden said, 'If ground, path and fruition are like
this, what fearless confidences do you have?'
In reply, Mila sang this song:

No gods and no demons is the confidence of the view.
Non-wandering and non–meditation is the confidence
    of meditation.
No hope and no fear is the confidence of fruition.
This yogin possesses these three confidences.
Would the young lady desire to realize these three
    confidences?

Thus, Mila sang.
With great faith, the maiden touched his feet. She invited
him in and offered him good hospitality. She requested
meditation instruction and offered this supplication:

O jetsun rinpoche,
O supreme yogin,
During the day, I am busy with work;
During the night, I fall into the sleep of delusion.
From dawn to dusk, I am the slave of food and clo-
    thing.
There is no time for practising Dharma.
I request the Dharma for attaining Buddhahood.
I request the Dharma for attaining enlightenment.

Thus, she sang.
    In reply, the jetsun sang this song of four analogies
and five meanings:

O young lady, Paldarbum,
Listen wealthy lady, endowed with faith.

Look up into the sky,
And practise meditation free from fringe and centre.
Look up at the sun and moon,
And practise meditation free from bright and dim.

Look over at the mountains,
And practise meditation free from departing and
    changing.

Look down at the lake,
And practise meditation free from waves.

Look here at your mind,
And practise meditation free from discursive thought.

Thus, Mila sang.
    The young lady meditated and later offered this examina-
tion of her mind:

O jetsun rinpoche,
O supreme yogin,

I am able to meditate on the sky;
But, when clouds arise, how should I meditate?

I am able to meditate on the sun and moon;
But when heavenly bodies move, how should I meditate?

I am able to meditate on the mountains;
But when trees and shrubbery blossom, how should I
  meditate?

I am able to meditate on the lake;
But when waves arise, how should I meditate?

I am able to meditate on the mind;
But when discursive thoughts occur, how should I
  meditate?

Thus, she sang.
  The jetsun sang this song to clear away her obstacles:

O young lady, Paldarbum,
Listen wealthy lady, endowed with faith.

If you are able to meditate on the sky,
Clouds are manifestations of the sky.
Once more resolve this manifestation;
Once more resolve your mind.

If you are able to meditate on the sun and moon,
The stars and planets are manifestations of the sun and
  moon.
Once more resolve this manifestation;
Once more resolve your mind.

If you are able to meditate on the mountains,
The trees and shrubbery are manifestations of the
  mountain.
Once more resolve this manifestation;
Once more resolve your mind.

If you are able to meditate on the lake,
The waves are manifestations of the lake.

Once more resolve this manifestation;
Once more resolve your mind.

If you are able to meditate on your mind,
Discursive thoughts are manifestations of your mind.
Once more examine the root of discursive thought;
Once more resolve your mind.

Thus, Mila sang.

The maiden meditated and excellent experiences came to her. Later the guru saw her again and sang this song of four encouraging counsels:

O young lady, Paldarbum,
Listen wealthy lady, endowed with faith.

The next life's journey is longer than this one.
Have you prepared provisions?

The provisions are generosity; do you have this?
The enemy known as miserliness causes obstructions;
It works seeming benefit, but will bring harm.
Do you know miserliness to be the enemy?
If you know this, cast it behind you.
If you understand this, cast it behind you.

O young lady, Paldarbum,
Listen wealthy lady, endowed with faith.

The next life is darker than this one.
Have you prepared a torch?
The torch is luminosity; do you meditate?
The enemy known as delusion is corpse-like sleep;
It works seeming benefit, but will bring harm.

Do you know delusion to be the enemy?
If you know this, cast it behind you.
If you understand this, cast it behind you.

O young lady, Paldarbum,
Listen wealthy lady, endowed with faith.

The next life is more fearful than this one.
Have you prepared a guide?
The guide is the divine Dharma; do you practise it?
The enemies known as relatives are hindrances;
They work seeming good, but will bring harm.
Do you know the relatives to be the enemy?
If you know this, cast them behind you.
If you understand this, cast them behind you.

O young lady, Paldarbum,
Listen wealthy lady, endowed with faith.

The next life's journey is longer and more perilous
    than this one's.
Have you prepared a stallion?
The stallion is exertion; have you mounted it?
The enemy known as laziness is sloth:

It works seeming benefit, but will bring harm.
Do you know laziness to be the enemy?
If you know this, cast it behind you.
If you understand this, cast it behind you.

Thus, Mila sang.

He gave her the oral instructions, she meditated, and became a wonderful yogini, holder of the hearing lineage.

This ends the chapter of Lhogo in Kungthang.

Part Four
The Nyingma Tradition

The Four-Themed Precious Garland
Longchen Rabjampa

Stainless meditation is done in a state of comprehending this Clear Light essence. It is free of mental darkness, agitation and fabrication, has no distraction and is beyond the conventional mind. It is great and extensive, completely pure like the sky. Unrestricted, not imbalanced by selectivity, it is totally beyond all thinking, speaking and conceptualizing.

Longchen Rabjampa

Introduction to Part Four

Milarepa's major disciple was the monk Gampopa. Before training in the tantric practices under Milarepa, Gampopa had studied with Kadampa teachers. He was an erudite scholar and a realized meditator who unified the approaches of both the Kagyu and Kadam traditions. As a condensation of his understanding of these two traditions, Gampopa's Four Themes provide an essential outline of the practice of Buddhism. These four are: (1) Turning the Mind to the Dharma; (2) Practising the Dharma as a Path; (3) Removing Confusion while on the path; and (4) Purifying Confusion into Pristine Awareness.

The text presented here is a commentary on these four themes by the renowned Nyingma teacher Longchen Rab-jampa. In his youth Longchenpa – as he is often called – received not only the transmissions of the Nyingma tradition but also those of the Kadam and Sakya schools. Like Gampopa, he produced extensive writings and was also an accomplished practitioner of meditation. The teachings he considered to represent the pinnacle of Buddhist thought and practice are those of Dzog-chen, which means 'The Great Completeness.' In his own words, the vehicle of Dzog-chen 'functions to bring you directly into the sphere of that which is spontaneously there. This sphere is unchanging .... It need not be sought because it is spontaneously present from time immemorial. No trying or effort [is required].' Not surprisingly, Dzog-chen has often been compared to the teachings of the Zen tradition.

In his treatment of the first two themes of Gampopa, Longchenpa outlines the contemplations which form the basis of all Buddhist traditions in Tibet. In his commentary to the third theme, *Removing Confusion while on the Path*, he introduces the interpretation of Dzog-chen. For further clarity this section also includes an oral commentary by His Holiness Dudjom Rinpoche, the present head of the Nyingma tradition. (This commentary appears here in indented paragraphs.) This third section also presents a summary of those tantric practices often regarded as a necessary basis for the insights of Dzog-chen.

The text was translated into English by Alexander Berzin in conjunction with Sherpa Tulku and Matthew Kapstein. It was published in 1979. Although the text of Longchen Rabjampa appears here in its entirety, parts of Dudjom Rinpoche's commentary have been slightly abridged. For reasons of space, a commentary to the fourth theme by Beru Khyentse Rinpoche, which appeared in the original edition, has been omitted.

Prologue

Homage to all the Buddhas and bodhisattvas.

With supreme hundred-fold faith I make offerings to you, O sun-like Buddhas. Your nature is the skylike expanse of your body that subsumes everything [Dharmakaya]. In it the [solar] mandala of your form body having five certainties bursts forth and causes lotus-like disciples to bloom by the rays of your deeds.

The cool shade of the precious wish-granting tree of the ways of the victorious ones' teachings [of the Dharma] offers protection from all the torments of samsaric life and complacent liberation. I shall therefore explain this massive tree of good qualities in four points as the way for all those with faith to enter step by step [into its shade]. Listen well.

1 *Turning Your Mind to the Dharma*

Whoever wishes to cross the boundless ocean of cyclic existence must first of all decide to make an effort now in this lifetime to achieve the peace and happiness which is the phenomenon of liberation. A human body, difficult to obtain and easily lost, is a raft of opportunities and endowments [for Dharma study and practice]. Having attained one, if you do not exert yourself [to take advantage of it], you will never be free from the ocean of samsaric life. You will never stop its flow of [lifetimes filled with] so many sufferings. You will be tossed about in the unbearable, fearsome great ocean [of samsara] where the tides of delusions extend to the highest realm, the form of sickness and old age is splashed everywhere and there is no visible end in sight to the current of birth and death.

But whoever hears the teachings will be able to stop the flow of birth and death and will never be parted from the supreme great bliss. Therefore, with the perfect, precious raft of the supreme Dharma [which brings] peace, make an effort to cross the ocean of the three realms' delusions.

If you do not practise the enlightening path to liberation now, in the future you will never even hear the words 'fortunate rebirth.' Through endless unfortunate lifetimes, one after the other, you will have no means of freeing yourself from cyclic existence. Therefore, now that you have attained a human body and endowments, those of you with sense should practise sincerely and with great effort what will bring you benefit and bliss. By means of this, you will be able to accomplish both your own and others' aims.

Even once you have attained the freedom and endowments, there is never any mental security, however. Everything is insecure, changes and has no essence. As all things are momentary, impermanent and will disintegrate, you should ponder in your heart how you will soon die.

It is the same with the whole world around you. It too will disintegrate by [the forces of] the seven fires, one flood and wind. Not even the single tip of a hair will remain. Everything will become empty; there will be only space. Those who live in it, impermanent fleeting beings – that is, gods, antigods, humans, animals, hungry ghosts and hell creatures – whatever sentient beings they are, when their time is up, they must plunge into the waters of death, transference of consciousness and rebirth. Years, months, days and divisions of time are momentary and impermanent, disintegrate and are [continually] passing. Just as the changing of the seasons is sad, think of how your own life will also be impermanent.

There is no mental security whatever. Very soon life will depart from your body. Therefore, from today on you must definitely think, 'It is entirely uncertain which will happen first, tomorrow, or the moment when my life span will be spent.'

The suffering of birth is more fearsome than that of death. There is never any happiness, no matter where you are born, for the nature of cyclic existence is like that of a blazing fire. Therefore, seek some method of becoming liberated from it right now.

Hell creatures are tormented by heat and cold, hungry ghosts by hunger and thirst, animals by devouring each other, by stupidity and ignorance, and human beings by the three and eight faults. Anti-gods [suffer from] fighting and war, gods from death, transference of consciousness and falling [to lower rebirths]. Their happiness can change to grief and their suffering of extensiveness is great. Once their consciousness has transferred from the pleasure and comfort of the god realms, they may enter the fires of hell once more. Thinking in this way, work to move beyond samsaric existence.

The appearances of this life are like your dreams just before you wake up: they are changing and impermanent. Since you must go and leave them behind, what can possessions, wealth and so on do for you? Make an effort in the Dharma right now.

Desire is like poison, weapons or fire. [Once it strikes] its torment is constant and there is no chance of happiness. [What is entailed is] the suffering of working to gather, protect and increase [what you desire and consequently] you are always bound by hoarding, stinginess and greed. In conflict with everyone, your defiled delusions increase. Your mind wanders, endlessly occupied, and it threatens your health and your existence.

Having too many involvements and activities contradicts your Dharma practice and is always despised by the noble ones, the aryas. If your desires are few, your virtuous actions will increase automatically. Therefore, you who wish to engage yourselves on the path to peaceful liberation, lessen your desires and be content.

It is said that if you exhaust your desires, you are a real arya and if your desires are few, you are nearly an arya. Just as suffering and delusions increase for those with desire, virtuous actions increase for those with little desire. Follow, therefore, in the footsteps of the holy masters of the past. Always be content and have few possessions.

The faults of being with other people are really limitless. There is far too much useless distraction and activity. Anger, arguments and conflict increase, and attraction and repulsion arise. You always become infected with their bad habits and this is pointless. No matter what you do, there is never a time when you can really please them. No matter how much you try, the chances are small that you can benefit them. No matter how much you listen to them, nothing good ever comes of it. No matter how close you are to someone, such as your best friend, in the end you will have to part. Therefore abandon all involvements in which you are dependent on followers, friends or relatives. Make a definite effort from today to live in quiet solitude in order to practise the pure Dharma.

Supreme holy beings of the past have said that whilst living in quietude they found the nectar [of Dharma experience]. Therefore resolve that you too shall live alone in a secluded forest in order to attain [a state of] peace.

Living in quietude has been praised by the Victorious Buddhas. With no one to annoy you, deep, singleminded concentration increases. You naturally practise the Dharma and sober thoughts of impermanence arise. Your possessions are put aside and you do not have the busyness of work or distractions. Masses of good qualities, such as faith and renunciation, multiply and, because there is no involvement with people, your activities automatically lessen.

Therefore, without the eight worldly feelings, not worrying about making others happy or about saving face, pass your days and nights with the Dharma in the bliss of having total freedom. [In this way] make your attainment of a fully-endowed body of freedom and endowments meaningful and take full advantage of it. As the benefits of all this are inexpressible, try to practise deep concentration your whole life, in complete solitude, in a forest.

May the cooling rain of the Dharma, fully explained in this way, extinguish the thought that is afflicted by delusion. May it fill the lotus pond of the collection of virtues of singleminded concentration. May it increase the attainment of the land of peace.

2 Practising the Dharma as a Path

Suppose that, by faith, you have entered the supreme, holy and virtuous Dharma and you now wish to go further, on a path to Liberation. [What you must do is to actually] put the Dharma into practice as a path [that is as a way of life]. This is essential in order to tame your mind.

There are those who have entered the teachings of the Victorious Buddhas in this way and have even embarked on a course of hearing, thinking about and meditating [on the teachings]. Yet some are not tranquil: they have base minds. Some pursue incorrect or inferior paths or ones that lead astray. Some have great desires and craving and some are distracted with concerns for this life. All such mistakes, contradictory to the Dharma, arise from not practising the Dharma as a path. The faults that come from this in this and future lives are immeasurable. Whoever is fooled by such deceptions will suffer regret at the time of death and will experience terror and anxiety in the in-between (bardo) period. They will go to a lower rebirth state in the future and never have the opportunity of becoming permanently liberated from cyclic existence. Therefore, practise the Dharma as a path.

Although people take medicine to cure their sickness, if

they do not take it properly, they may become sicker than before. Likewise, what use is the Dharma if it is not followed properly as a cure? Therefore, since there are limitless problems such as this, those of you with faith should understand this well.

Practising the Dharma as a path depends, firstly, on your spiritual master. It is therefore important to rely on a holy, fully-qualified Guru. Whatever good qualities there are come from this.

As for him, he should be someone with compassion and skilful means, who is tranquil, has self-control and is patient. His vows, word of honour and mode of behaviour should be perfect and binding. He should have heard many [teachings] and should have practised them well. His waves of inspiration should be measureless, automatically influencing the appearance of others. He should be unconcerned with this life and cleansed like the sky of the eight worldly feelings. Such a person, who makes the life of anyone associated with him meaningful and places them on a path to liberation, is a form of victorious ones manifested at the time of the deteriorations. Therefore, devote yourself perfectly, with great respect.

The benefits from this are measureless and inexhaustible. You become disgusted with samsaric existence and renounce it. Thus, your thoughts for this life lessen. In your mind you let go of [concern] for this life and your grasping for true identities based on deceptive appearances falls away. You will naturally have self-control and will hear, think about and meditate [on the teachings]. You will acquire extensive good qualities, such as faith. Your present life will become meaningful and your future ones will reap the results. Therefore devote yourself to a holy [master].

Moreover, you should never be dishonest with the three gates [of your body, speech and mind]. Be like a patient to his doctor, a merchant [travelling on the sea] to his navigator, a passenger to his oarsman, a guest to his escort. Try always to please him by respectful service. It is taught that if you develop a disrespectful [attitude] or distorted view [of him], you enter a hellish rebirth for [as many aeons as] the number of moments [you develop it]. Therefore protect, as you would your eyes, your various words of honour [to respect him]. Do this by confessing [if you ever violate them], restraining yourself and feeling great regret [should you ever break them].

Devote yourself in this way to a supreme spiritual master and cultivate your mind-stream by hearing, thinking about and meditating on [his teachings]. Then, intentionally transform whatever you do into virtue with the thought of desiring only liberation. This is an oral tradition teaching on how to practise the Dharma as a path.

Whenever you listen [to the teachings], think about or recite them, undertake these for the sake of liberating your mind-stream. Whenever you write, read, memorize or teach, do so desiring only liberation. In your meditation, philosophizing and conduct, too, try to feel strong renunciation and disgust with samsara by never separating your mind from being set on liberation alone. There is nothing higher than these essential oral teachings.

Eating, sleeping, walking, sitting, talking, speaking, thinking and so on – in short, whatever activity you are doing, never let your mind stray from the wish for liberation. Develop disgust [with samsara] and thus tame your mind-stream. This is the essential point for practising the Dharma as a path.

Furthermore, to travel the Mahayana path in particular, you should dedicate whatever virtuous actions you do for the sake of others. Thus, in order to benefit sentient beings, you should wholeheartedly practise developing a compassionate enlightened motive of bodhicitta, having fervent regard [for enlightenment and helping others], dedicating [your merit] and rejoicing [in your own and others' virtues]. In this connection [you should recognize that in previous lives] all beings have been your mother and father, relatives and dear friends. It is thus fitting that they should receive your help.

You yourself must develop an enlightened motive for the sake of others. Then practise virtue for the benefit of all beings. By your virtuous actions, others will become happy. You should cultivate and enhance your enlightened motive with immeasurable compassion by thinking. 'May everyone's suffering ripen on me and may my virtuous actions ripen on them. May all beings attain Buddhahood.'

Whatever virtuous actions you do, precede them by the development of an enlightened motive, carrry them out without objectifying anything and conclude them by dedicating the merit. Also, you should completely purify (yourself of misconceptions about the true nature of] the three spheres – the object of what is to be practised, what is being practised and the one who is practising. Like illusions, they are mere appearances [based] on nothing real – like magical creations. Therefore, purifying the natures [of these three], you should dedicate the merit in order to benefit others.

True respect means having deep faith in the victorious Buddhas, their Dharma teachings, their holy [bodhisattva] sons and daughters and in the objects for accumulating merit – in all these, without exception. From having regard to benefiting yourself, others and both [yourself and others], you will receive praise, respect and esteem beyond all example.

Rejoicing is meditating on the happiness of all the virtuous acts of the Buddhas, bodhisattvas and all beings. This is a supreme method for transforming limitless masses of merit into great immeasurable [pristine awareness].

Pure prayers should be offered in order to benefit beings. For this the oral tradition teaching of purifying the objects of your practice should be meditated upon.

Never be distracted for even a moment by ordinary things. Take as your essential practice working for others and making virtue with the three gates [of your body, speech and mind]. To tame your mind-stream in order to thoroughly develop an enlightened motive is said to be the way to make any practice of Dharma into a path [to enlightenment].

In this way may the melodious beat of the sound of the drum of the profound meaning, the well-known sweet roar which is both vast and profound, wake all beings from the intoxication and sleep of their ignorance. May they see a joyous festival of peace for ever.

3 Removing Confusion while on the Path

Furthermore, there are common, special and peerless methods for removing confusion while on the path. The first of these is the great Mahayana path [of the sutras] which is followed in common [by all Mahayana traditions]. On this path you cultivate an enlightened motive of bodhicitta [on the basis of] the four immeasurables. Thus endowed with prayer and compassion, you eliminate confusion [that might impede your progress] by working exuberantly [for others]. With [bodhicitta which has] the nature of voidness and compassion, you will be able to fulfil completely the purpose of yourself and others.

In order to cleanse fleeting stains from the void sphere of all things, which is in itself virtuous and unconditioned, you must meditate on the thirty-seven facets of the path to perfection while on the paths of accumulation, preparation, seeing and meditation.

[In addition] you must fully realize the pure, correct view of the sixteen types of voidness and complete the faultless practice of the six perfections. And [in particular for the perfection of wisdom] you must understand the identitylessness of both the conventional 'I' and all phenomena. Using these methods as an antidote, cleanse yourself of the moral and mental defilements. This is the supreme path of bodhisattvas.

Although everything only exists [on the conventional level] in the form of mirages, dreams and deceptive appearances, you should abandon and adopt [appropriate practices on the paths to enlightenment], work for the sake of others, avoid (non-virtuous actions] and undertake [virtuous ones]. Cleanse yourself of the defilements of longing desire, fearful and angered repulsion and closed-mindedness with the waters of [their antidotes, namely meditation on] ugliness, love and interdependent origination.

Because the ultimate level of truth is unborn and pure, it is without such dualistic [distinctions] as samsara and nirvana. It is free from such mental fabrications [of the conventional mind]. This is the meaning of the two truths. This path of interdependent origination is the causal Mahayana vehicle of philosophical studies.

The special Mahayana path of the secret tantras has outer and inner [divisions]. It has the fathomlessly supreme method of the unity of the development and completing stages by which you cleanse away confusion through various stages.

> Both the development and completing stages of tantra entail various practices for eliminating impure, deceptive cognition obscuring the path. The former involves complex visualizations and the latter meditation on voidness. It is insufficient to merely practise one of these stages by itself. The visualizations should not be taken as concrete; you must recognize that their foundation is voidness. Furthermore, voidness should not be taken nihilistically as denying everything. It does not impede interdependent origination. Thus, the unity of the development and completing stages means their simultaneous practice – not doing one without the other.

In the three outer classes of tantra, the main emphasis is on purification. You should abandon and adopt in turn [what is appropriate] and thus eliminate taints by [applying their] antidotes.

> On the level of practice of the three outer tantras – kriya, carya and yoga – you are unable as yet to transform delusions or defilements into pristine awareness. Therefore you abandon the former and adopt the latter. You apply direct opponents or antidotes to the moral and mental defilements such as the purifying practices of ritual ablution and annointment, meditation on love and compassion, and so forth.
>
> To practise these in turn means to apply whichever antidote is necessary in terms of whatever tainting defilement is absent or present in a given situation. Because the path is conceived in terms of defilements to be cleansed and opposing antidotes to cleanse them, there is this application in turn. These outer tantras are quite difficult to practise.

As for the inner [tantras], through pristine awareness, which is an undivided unity, those things to be abandoned become the path through [the application of] means.

> The inner tantras are those of maha-, anu- and atiyoga. In their practice you realize pristine awareness, which is an undivided unity of method and wisdom – in other words, the unity of relative and ultimate realities from the point of view of this unity's being a cognitive function. Through the totality of this pristine awareness those thing to be abandoned, such as the defilements together with their suffering, are utilized, when they arise, as aspects of the path through the application of appropriate means. This does not

mean that you encourage the arising of defiled
states of mind. Rather, there is no need for the
deliberate action of 'abandoning' delusions; they
are automatically transcended with such awareness. This is the distinctive feature of the three
higher tantras.

All things appear naturally on the mandala, which is the
foundation expanse, the Buddha-nature, and do so merely
through your own mind.

Ultimate reality is the mandala of the perfectly
pure expanse of voidness. It is like a magic mirror. What unimpededly appears on it are the
things [dharmas] of relative reality, your mind
included. These things appear naturally on this
'magic' mirror, through and to your mind. There
is no third reality of a truly existing mind or
objects juxtaposed to the ultimate reality of the
mirror and the relative reality of the images in it.

They are confusing deceptions and do not really exist.
They are void forms which nevertheless appear distinctly as
the aggregate physical and mental faculties, the cognitive
bases and spheres, and so forth. Seen purely, they are the
Buddha-families, and so on.

All phenomena of relative reality are void by
nature. Deceptively, they appear truly to exist,
but do not really do so. Yet from voidness various
distinct appearances do arise, for instance, forms.
They are reflections of the 'magic' mirror, voidness, and appear distinctly as your aggregates and
as the consciousness, cognitive power and objects
of your mind and senses. With pure vision you
experience them in a subtler manner. You regard
your five aggregate faculties as the five 'dhyani'
Buddhas, your five bodily elements [earth,
water, fire, air and space] as the five consorts,

your eight types of consciousness [foundation, defiled, mental and the five sensory] as the eight meditational bodhisattvas, and so forth. Thus, your entire body and all your defilements are regarded as having a divine nature.

Thus, on the development stage, all that appears is united into a single mandala. Bodies become deities, speech becomes mantra, and memories and thoughts are applied to emanating and absorbing [pristine awareness. In this way] ordinary deceptive appearances are regarded as a Buddha-field.

Relative things ordinarily appear to be concrete. This is deceptive because in actuality they lack true existence. When this confusing deception is transcended with pristine awareness, things are experienced in a wholly different, subtler manner. From the viewpoint of the unity of voidness and appearance, everything is in fact a perfect Buddha-field − a mandala filled with deities. There is nothing there that can still be referred to as a 'deceptive appearance.'

All bodies and speech encountered become deities and mantras through this pure type of vision. Whatever thoughts or memories occur are seen as the play of pristine awareness through visualizing such awareness in various forms emanating from you and then re-absorbing. This whole practice, in which there is the necessity to transform body, speech and mind into deities, mantras and so forth in order to eliminate confusion about them, is the path of the development stage.

Through [the procedures of] the completing stage, you enter the inconceivable sphere of clear light in which everything is in the state of its actual void nature. [This is accomplished] through the yoga methods dealing with the energy-channels, energy-currents and creative energies. Your consciousness and energy-currents come under your control and become usable.

> On the completing stage of the inner tantras you treat your body as energy-channels [nadi], your speech as energy-currents [prana] and your mind as creative energy [bindu]. While practising the yoga methods concerning these energy-systems, meditate on the nature of the mind as pristine awareness characterized by great bliss. As a result, these currents of energy become usable to achieve the ordinary and extraordinary powerful attainments [siddhi]. There are many examples of master practitioners [mahasiddha] of the past who have performed miraculous deeds because of their mastery of such methods. These may be found in historical accounts.

The spheres of voidness and pristine awareness become conjoined. The indivisible unity [which is their conjunction] is the path of mahamudra. This is the resultant Vajrayana vehicle of the secret tantras.

> Through the above techniques you realize the unity of voidness and pristine awareness or, in other words, of voidness and its unimpeded play. Thus you attain a Buddha's body of pristine awareness [jnanakaya], the cognitive aspect of the body of the essential nature [svabhavakaya] – this latter being the abiding nature of all reality. Because Buddhahood is understood to be identical with this abiding nature, there is no need to deal with the causes of its arising. Rather, emphasis is placed on cultivating the realization of this reality. Thus the mahamudra path of the tantras continually deals with its result or aim, the state of Buddhahood, and therefore is referred to as the resultant path.

The yoga of the energy-channels and others is the foremost feature of anu-yoga. It is also practised in ati-yoga, just as ati- is in maha-yoga. In fact, all three inner tantras are mutually pervasive, incorporating aspects of each other. A certain practice is classified as maha-, anu- or ati-yoga in reference to what is emphasized or is foremost in it. The main feature of a maha-yoga practice is the development stage, that of anu-yoga is the completing stage, while that of ati-yoga or dzog-chen is the cultivation of the realization of the void sphere of all things. Each of these practices, however, has development [maha], completing [anu] and dzog-chen [ati] stages. For the purpose of theoretical exposition, it is easier to understand if these three inner tantras are treated separately.

For example, in a maha-yoga practice you begin with meditation on voidness, seeing everything purified into the void. From this state arise exuberant waves of the motivation of compassion. This is called 'single-pointed concentration appearing everywhere.' When the unity of voidness and compassion is established through such meditation, it is called 'single-minded concentration on suchness.'

In this state the arising of pure awareness is practised through meditation on a visualized seed syllable such as HUM. Rays of light stream from it, purifying the entire environment of samsara and the beings within it. All are realized as being of the nature of voidness. Through this process the world becomes a Buddha-field, or the divine realm of a meditational deity, buildings become the celestial palace of the deity and your mind becomes the seed syllable. If this syllable is HUM, then at the next stage it becomes a vajra or lightning-sceptre of the enlightened motive of bodhicitta. From this vajra, light streams out and this in turn becomes the meditational deity, for instance Vajrasattva. Proceeding thus through many extensive stages, you practise the development stage of maha-yoga tantra.

In an anu-yoga practice the above stages are somewhat abbreviated. The prime emphasis is on the mastery of the yoga dealing with the energy-channels, energy-currents and creative energies.

Ati-yoga or dzog-chen is often known as 'maha-ati.' Here 'maha' refers to the practice of a development stage as in maha-yoga. 'Maha' literally means 'great' and 'ati,' 'most.' Realization of the abiding nature of reality is the highest or most supreme practice.

The reason why a maha-yoga development stage must be conjoined with an anu- or ati-yoga practice is as follows. If you have not meditated to at least a certain extent on a visualization of Guru Rinpoche or some other deity , reciting his mantra, you will have nothing upon which to base your practice of an anu-yoga completing stage. You will lack a context within which to meditate on the energy-system and voidness. Likewise, if you have not trained yourself with a development stage practice of deliberately visualizing a deity and reciting a mantra, you will have no background or basis enabling you in ati-yoga to experience everything spontaneously as a perfect mandala, deity, and so forth. Thus, the three inner tantras are not practised separately.

The supreme peerless vehicle of the secret dzog-chen, the great completeness, functions to bring you directly into the sphere of that which is spontaneously there. This sphere, which is the foundation, is unchanging. All good qualities [appear] in it spontaneously as the sun, moon, planets and stars do in the sky. It need not be sought for because it is spontaneously present from time immemorial. No effort [is required]. This path is natural and self-evident.

> The foundational sphere or 'founding stratum,' which exists primordially, is identical with pure awareness. It never changes and is thus likened to the sky or space. In this space the various Buddha bodies, qualities and pristine awareness arise spontaneously, just as the sun, moon and stars appear in the sky, without being sought for. The planets and stars to not come about through your efforts, yet you can see them. Likewise, without deliberate effort, you can directly perceive the obvious path of voidness, because voidness by nature is directly perceivable. Dzog-chen, then, is the path of voidness itself.

The mandala sphere of clear light is unconditioned. It is the innate Dharmakaya, the all-pervasive intentionality [of the Buddhas]. To realize it directly is the supreme view of reality.

> The nature of voidness is clear light, which is pure and present from time immemorial. The mandala of that sphere of clear light is unconditioned by causes and circumstances. It is the innate dharmakaya, the unconditioned abiding nature of all things, inherent in the mind-streams of all sentient beings. Thus, the foundational sphere of the clear light of voidness within everyone's mind-stream is as all-pervasive as space.
>
> The dharmakaya is the body [kaya] that subsumes all things [dharmas] that can be perceived and expressed by a Buddha. It is the knowledge that directly perceives the ultimate nature of the void sphere of all things and is the direct cause of

a Buddha's accomplishing unsurpassed benefits for all sentient beings.

The Buddha-nature is voidness or the dharmakaya, from the point of view of its being the inherent potential of Buddhahood. It is innate within the mind-stream of all sentient beings. Samantabhadra is the dharmakaya personified as the primordial Buddha [Adi-Buddha]. The mind of Samantabhadra is a synonym for the intentionality of the Buddhas and is the inherent awareness that fully realizes its own enlightened state. In other words, although primordial awareness of the abiding nature of reality is inherent in the mind-streams of all sentient beings, they are unaware of it. It is shrouded in ignorance or, literally, in 'unawareness.' Samantabhadra, however, is aware of his own enlightened state. When you likewise become aware of your own innate condition, you recover the mind of Samantabhadra. To realize directly this all-pervasive intentionality of the Buddhas, the mind of Samantabhadra, is the supreme view of reality, according to dzog-chen. It is based on directly introducing the disciple to the innate dharmakaya within his own mind-stream.

On the sphere that is perfectly pure there are clouds of fleeting obscurations. These are deceptive appearances [projected by] the minds of sentient beings. Through these appearances, based on nothing real, the three realms and six classes of beings are perpetuated.

The void sphere of all things is perfectly pure, free from all mental fabrications. On it, the ignorant mind projects ephemeral taints in the manner of clouds obscuring the sky. When these taints of ignorance or unawareness obscure the sphere of voidness, there appear the abodes of the three realms [desire, form and formless] and the six classes of beings [hell creatures, hungry ghosts, animals, humans, anti-gods and gods]. In other words, these taints appear as the realms and beings of samsara, although they have no real existence of their own. These appearances arise from deception and confusion, and because of them sentient beings wander from one physical abode to another, continuously.

The Buddha-nature is the actual nature of Samantabhadra inherent in everyone from time immemorial. It pervades all beings. The mind of Samantabhadra is compared with the sky, because it is all-pervasive. Such a mind perceives the void nature of all things and recognizes this as its own true nature. It sees its own void nature in all things as if seeing itself in a mirror. Therefore, the mind of Samantabhadra is said 'to recognize by itself its own face.'

When beings do not recognize themselves in this way, their innate dharmakaya or Buddha-nature becomes for them an 'alaya' or 'foundation of everything.' At this stage because there is not yet any grasping at a differentiation of objects within that foundation, it is still likened to the sky and is characterized by bliss and voidness. In other words, when you fail to see the dharmakaya as your own nature, that dharmakaya becomes for you an 'alaya' – the source of everything of both samsara and nirvana. However, it is not yet actively producing these things. It is the potential for this process and this is undifferentiated.

From the play of that alaya foundation there arises the sort of unawareness or ignorance that causes you to think of yourself as a single, unique individual. This subtle cognition that thinks 'I am' is known as self-preoccupation. From it arises the consciousness grasping for 'I' and 'mine' which thinks to grasp or draw things to itself in order to establish or prove its own existence. It is through this process that graspable objects arise.

If at this stage you simply let go the arising of graspable objects – leaving them the moment they arise without pursuing them or trying to prove anything – the process terminates. All that has arisen subsides and dissolves. But if they are not let go, there is the further arising of specific sensory consciousnesses and the identification that 'this consciousness is grasping this object' and 'that consciousness is grasping that one.' With this ensues the process of naming and giving meaning to those names. This is how grasping formulates.

Thus, once the idea of 'I' and 'mine' has arisen, the entire mechanism of sense objects and consciousness, or subject and object, proceeds in order to gratify the acquisitiveness of this imagined 'I' through concrete sensory experiences. The imagined 'I' tries to make itself feel real by creating and pursuing sensory experiences. This is a brief description of how grasping consciousness and grasped-at objects arise, producing and perpetuating samsara.

Whenever anything appears, no matter what it is, it is non-existent on the ultimate level. Like clouds in the sky, these appearances [come and go] merely because of fleeting circumstances. Therefore, samsara is overestimated. In actual nature, it falls apart.

Sentient beings grasp as being real all objects and moments of consciousness produced through the above process. However, if examined thoroughly, their true nature is voidness. Ultimately, nothing can be found. Everything of relative reality appears through ever-changing momentary causes, like clouds in the sky.

When moisture in the air is moved about by the wind, clouds are formed in the sky. But since clouds are the manifestations of the wind and moisture of the sky, it is impossible to conceive of them as being really different or separate from it. They have no other place to go to establish their existence. Clouds can only gather in the sky and then vanish from it.

In the same way, the deceptive appearances generated by your mind's unawareness or ignorance produce the three realms and the six types of beings. The mind is like the moisture, unawareness like the wind, the various realms and deceptive appearances are like the clouds and the sky is the Buddha-nature. The mind, as a cognitive possibility, is inherent in the Buddha-nature in the same way as moisture is inherent in the atmosphere. Driven by the winds of ignorance, the deceptive appearances of samsara gather as clouds. The force that causes the dissolution of these appearances is awareness, that is awareness that none of these appearances is beyond having voidness as its nature. There is no other place for these appearances to be fabricated from than voidness, nor is there any other place for them to go.

To think, therefore, that samsara has true existence is an overestimation or interpolation. It imagines existing that which in fact does not. Samsara's three realms are merely an appearance, based on nothing real. They are created by the interpolation that 'there is this' and 'there is that,' and subsequently you grasp at your own interpolations. When you realize their actual nature, they naturally disperse, like clouds from the sky.

Although not really existent, things still appear. From their own side, however [such things] are void by nature. These void appearances do not actually exist. They are like a blur or falling hairs [seen by someone with cataract], or like a dream, a mirage or a conchshell perceived as yellow [by someone with jaundice]. From time immemorial such appearances have never been [validly] experienced as existing in the manner in which they appear. They have no foundation, no support, no beginning, middle or end. You must realize that from primordial time everything by nature is pure.

Thus, whether they be samsaric appearances, sentient beings, the environment, or whatever – there are no [outer] objects [for consciousness] to grasp. They are like magical creations or visual apparitions. Also, in just the same way, there is no [inner] consciousness to grasp anything. All is pure – like empty space. As both consciousness and its objects do not really exist, samsara has never been experienced as being existent. By realizing that it is a deceptive appearance and by nature not really existent, you become liberated from it.

> When you realize the abiding nature of all things, there is no other course but liberation, namely through the dissolution of the clouds of deceptive appearance, leaving you with the void sky of your Buddha-nature.

Things to be abandoned or adopted, causes, effects and circumstances are all appearances. Since they themselves are pure, you must realize that the actual nature of reality on the ultimate level is beyond all cause and effect.

The foundation or support for this [realization] is pure awareness or ultimate bodhicitta.

> When you ascertain the actual abiding nature of all things and arrive at voidness, there is no longer anything that can be labelled or spoken of. Then

the objection may arise, 'If this is the case, then how can the ultimate be known or realized?' The answer is that at this point there is pure awareness, also known as ultimate bodhicitta or pristine awareness. This is voidness from the point of view of its being realized, taking into consideration that voidness transcends the division into consciousness and an object. Thus it is a way of talking about voidness as if it had a cognitive aspect. To be beyond the division into subject and object does not render voidness as something unrealizable, nor the realizer of voidness an inanimate object without any consciousness.

This is the sphere of [natural] nirvana, the great spontaneity, the ultimate level of truth, primordially pure. It has a nature with neither a beginning nor an end. It is clear light by nature – profound, tranquil and free of mental fabrication. It is [pristine awareness], innate within you since time immemorial, the taintless dharmakaya. It abides as an actuality free from change and transition through the three times [past, present and future]. This is the foundational sphere, the vajra essence of reality. Whoever understands it realizes the correct view of the abiding nature of reality. With over- and under-estimation pacified, you understand the essence of ultimate reality.

To overestimate reality is to interpolate that it is truly existent, when in fact it is not. Underestimating it is to repudiate or deny its relative existence, for it nevertheless does appear. Therefore the understanding of ultimate and relative realities – the two levels of truth – is a middle path devoid of extremes.

This concludes the discussion of the correct dzog-chen view. Next is shown how to cultivate that view through meditation.

Stainless meditation is done in a state of comprehending this clear light essence. It is free of mental dullness, agitation and fabrication, has no distraction and is beyond the conventional mind. It is great and extensive, completely pure like the sky. Unrestricted, not imbalanced by selectivity, it is totally beyond all thinking, speaking and conceptualizing.

> In the *Bodhicaryavatara* Shantideva writes, 'Ultimate reality is not within the range of conventional mind.' Having, in your meditation, gone beyond the relative objects of such a mind, you are in an unrestricted state transcending the selective process of 'This is this' and 'That is that.' There are no objects to be analyzed or examined and there is no basis for mental wandering. After all, who is the one who is mentally wandering and where are the objects to wander after? You have already arrived at voidness. This meditational state, therefore, is beyond thinking, speaking and conceptualizing because there are no conventional objects to think or speak about on the ultimate level. It is beyond mental dullness as well because the nature of the ultimate is clear light and pristine awareness.

> Having completed the topics of the correct view and meditation, what follows is how to act based on that view.

As for activity, whatever appears has no truth and is perfectly pure. Thus, whatever internal grasping thoughts arise naturally dissolve.

> No matter what thoughts arise during your daily conduct, if you recognize their true nature, they have no other course than naturally to subside. In the same way as pictures are drawn on water, thoughts that arise do so on the surface of pure awareness and must dissolve again back into

the same awareness. But this is not to say that in the process the causes for their arising simply vanish. Thoughts continue to arise at this stage, but dissolve as soon as they do. They are not pursued.

If there were no further arising of thoughts, this state would become the same as the cessation of suffering taught by the Hinayana Shravakas. Without any movement, they achieve a complete cessation. But this is not the dzog-chen method. Instead of trying to bring the conventional thought process to a complete standstill, as a dzog-chen practitioner you learn to recognize the true nature of your thoughts. As soon as they arise you see them for what they are and they naturally subside.

External objects grasped at are like a dream or a mirage. Ultimately, neither [consciousness nor objects] are real. Therefore act without either undertaking or rejecting.

Ultimately, nothing to be undertaken or rejected can be established as having true existence. Therefore, right action based on the correct view of voidness is beyond the rigid categories of accepting and abandoning.

Whatever arises – either objects or consciousness, defilements, cessations or affirmations – naturally dissolve as soon as it occurs. That is to say, once its true nature is known, it dissolves. And this dissolution is into a state of dharmakaya, which has been complete from time immemorial, pervading everything equally. Therefore, having abandoned samsara, there is no need to search for nirvana.

As explained above, when you do not recognize your innate Buddha-nature, then the dharmakaya becomes for you an alaya foundation. With the subtle cognition of self-preoccupation, this foundation gives rise to thoughts and objects. If you recognize them for what they are and do not indulge yourself in the further processes of differentiation, selectivity and so forth, these thoughts and objects naturally dissolve back into the dharmakaya awareness of voidness. There is nowhere else for them to go, like clouds dispersing in the sky. It is in this way, then, that you abandon the samsaric cycle of grasping consciousness and grasped-at objects without needing to seek a Shravaka's nirvana of total cessation of conventional thought.

Whatever [objects] appear they are like mirrors reflecting the ultimate. Whatever [states of consciousness] arise, they naturally dissolve as soon as they are recognized. This is the play of the dharmakaya. Like water and waves, they are one continuum in the dharmakaya. This is the significance of the ultimate meaning, the very summit of views, the great completeness, dzog-chen.

Whatever objects appear, they are to be seen as mirrors. Since their nature is the clear light of voidness, they reflect the ultimate, while their conventional appearance is left unimpeded.

Whatever thoughts arise, they are to be recognized as coming from voidness and naturally dissolving back into it. They are the play of the dharmakaya. Like waves and water, never separate from each other, your rising and ebbing thoughts are one continuum with your dharmakaya.

Thus, looking at an object, you can see reflected in its voidness your innate dharmakaya and in its appearance your thoughts – the play of the dharmakaya.

In short, however you practise [the most important points are] the natural dissolution of ego-grasping and the purification of delusions in the sphere [of the dharmakaya]. Whoever is skilled in the practice of all these means achieves what is called the removal of confusion while on the path.

By [sailing] the precious great ship of this form of teaching, may all sentient beings without exception cross the ocean of samsara. On the supreme island of precious, peaceful liberation, may they realize a festival of unending peace and bliss.

4 Purifying Confusion into Pristine Awareness

Next comes the purification of confusion into pristine awareness. Of the two stages for this, the provisional and ultimate, the first is the provisional. This deals with the time when you are practising on the paths. By familiarizing yourself with profound methods, you will be able to purify whatever delusions arise into their own sphere. To make manifest pristine awareness which is the natural clarity [of the mind] is called purifying confused thoughts into the sphere of pristine awareness.

This can be further divided according to the methods relied upon on the common, special and peerless [paths. These are respectively] cleansing [confusing delusions] with their antidotes, transforming them with methods and purifying them into the sphere [of pristine awareness] without abandoning them since they naturally dissolve in their own way. Regardless of how you train yourself, with whatever type of purifying [method] you like, the state of cessation and that of purification of the delusions are ultimately the same.

When you recognize the natural ground for the arising of desire, anger, closed-mindedness, pride and jealousy [you see that] they automatically settle. They naturally dissolve, purified as the five aspects of pristine awareness.

This is known as the provisional purification of the confusion of the five poisons into the major pristine awareness, namely, the analytic, mirror-like, sphere of voidness, equalizing and accomplishing.

As for the ultimate [attainment], when you remove the fleeting stains from the expanse [of the Buddha-nature] and discover the peaceful, spotless state of Perfection, the nature of this sphere becomes manifest just as it is. The three Buddha bodies, dharmakaya, single taste or pristine awareness that you discover is known as the body of the sphere [of voidness] possessing double purity. This is not an object [known] by anyone other than the Buddhas.

The three Buddha bodies, namely the body that subsumes everything [dharmakaya], the utility body [sambhogakaya] and emanation body [nirmanakaya], together with pristine awareness, are all incorporated into the body of the essential nature [svabhavakaya], which is permanent, all-pervasive, unconditioned and without movement or change. Abiding in the sphere of the dharmakaya, which is a wish-fulfilling gem, the body of the virtuous conduct of pristine awareness arises from this state as the utility and emanation bodies which appear respectively to those on the bodhisattva stages and to other sentient beings. However, they only appear like that through the conjunction of the force of the Buddhas' waves of inspiration and the merit of those to be tamed. The [attainment of a] Buddha's virtuous conduct which, as long as samsara endures, continues uninterruptedly to fulfil the wishes [of all sentient beings] like a wish-granting tree or gem is known as the [ultimate] purification of confusion into pristine awareness.

May the seven-horse-drawn sun, which is the essence of the profound meaning [explained] like this, shed thousands of light-rays of its various words and their meanings on the world of disciples through the pathway of the sky of their minds and thus eliminate the darkness of ignorance from all beings.

Author's Colophon

This joyous feast of the methods [of these teachings], which has been spread for the sake of both myself and others from the excellent house of broad intelligence and enriched with a wealth of hearing, thinking and meditating, has been arranged in accordance with the meaning of the sutras, tantras and essential oral teachings. By the virtue of this, may I and all sentient beings level the mountain of samsara in this lifetime and attain the supreme peaceful and spotless state of enlightenment. May we become Buddhas and completely accomplish the aims of ourselves and others. And then, in a land adorned with immense snow-mountains of clear meaning, may the sum of our white virtuous qualities, which extends to the limit of all directions, highlight points on the treasure-field of the scriptures, thereby bringing joy to the masses of beings with faith.

This work, called *The Four-Themed Precious Garland*, has been completed by the yogi of the supreme vehicle, Kunkyab Ngaggi Wangpo [Longchen Rabjampa, 1308–1363] in one sitting by the light of the waxing crystal moon in the excellent house of Samantabhadra within the grove called A Cloud of Flowers on the slopes of Limestone Mountain. May a rain of great bliss fall for all times and in all directions as in the Golden Age, fulfilling all the hopes and wishes made by everyone.

Part Five
The Geluk Tradition

A Brief Exposition of the Stages on the Path to Enlightenment
Tsongkhapa

Ah, isn't it wonderful to have had the good fortune of attaining a human form fully endowed with the leisures and opportunities for Dharma study and of meeting with the teaching of the Buddha's Dharma. Now we should make our fully-endowed bodies, from which we can achieve the highest goals, effective for doing so by practising the Dharma day and night. What intelligent person would be satisfied with only partial results?

Tsongkhapa

Introduction to Part Five

Tsongkhapa, the founder of the Geluk tradition, wrote this short text as a letter to a friend and disciple, Konchog Tsultrim. Konchog Tsultrim had written, asking for advice on the practice of tantra. In response, Tsongkhapa gave a brief but thorough presentation of his view of the stages on the path to enlightenment. He begins by stressing the importance of relying on a qualified teacher or guru, and outlining the different motivations that impel people to practise Buddhism. After summarizing the preparatory practices such as the taking of refuge and the cultivation of the mind of enlightenment, he gives a clear introduction to the visualization practices of the first of the two stages of supreme yoga tantra, the development stage. His presentation of the completion stage, however, is extremely brief. The text concludes with a clear, detailed account of the Madhyamika philosophy of emptiness.

Prior to formulating his own understanding of the Buddhist teachings, Tsongkhapa studied widely with masters of the Nyingma, Sakya and Kagyu schools. Several characteristic features of Tsongkhapa's resultant synthesis are evident in this text. There is much emphasis on the need for a sound moral and intellectual foundation before proceeding with either the advanced practices of the tantras or the single-pointed meditation on emptiness. For Tsongkhapa, the successful practice of any stage along the path rests firmly on the successful accomplishment of the preceding stages. A meticulous scholar, Tsongkhapa also felt it important to trace back and present the Indian Buddhist source material on which his teachings were based. Yet, although his extensive scholarship is demonstrated by this example of his writing, there is a constant emphasis on the need to integrate any intellectual understanding through sustained meditation.

The text was translated into English under the title *A Brief Exposition of the Main Points of the Graded Sutra and Tantra Courses to Enlightenment* by Sherpa Tulku, Khamlung Tulku, Alexander Berzin and Jonathan Landaw. This is a revised edition of the translation that was published in 1975.

1 *Preliminary Practices*

Salutations to Guru Manjushri!

May I always be cared for by you, O Exalted One, my peerless teacher. Your stainless understanding of even the most detailed teachings never falters. This is due to your long experience of teaching, effective methods, the profound insight of *shunyata* and the widespread action of bodhicitta: the enlightened motive of working to attain Buddhahood in order to be able to liberate all living beings from their suffering.

O my great teacher, first you sought acquaintance with the many scriptures. Then, having pondered their meaning and understood it, you spread the Dharma with perfect exposition. Finally, you meditated enthusiastically for a long time, putting all the teachings into practice. May your feet be firmly planted on the ground throughout a long life.

I have received the perfect, sweet tree of your letter, together with its fruit of your presents which you sent, my dear friend, out of your kind thoughts for me. Not being satisfied by the good explanations and expositions you have already received, as an ocean cannot be satisfied by a cloudful of rain, you have asked me to write to you further concerning the two stages of tantra practice. A mind of small understanding can easily be filled by a single, rushing stream of water. Thus it is awe-inspiring that the minds of teachers of great understanding like you are so vast that they cannot be satisfied even by the wonderful accounts of the teachings already available.

However, granted that this may be so, it is quite impossible for the minds of great men like you to be satisfied by someone like myself. I have heard and read few teachings. My understanding is small; my practice is weak. Although I may have a few words to say, I have been very lax in meditating on their meaning. Nevertheless, dandelion seeds, propelled by the wind, can soar to compete with the birds, even though they lack the power to do so by themselves. Similarly, propelled by the ennobling words of great teachers like you, I shall offer here a few brief explanations.

You have found a human form fully endowed with the leisure to study the Dharma. You have met with the jewel-like teachings of Buddha, have obtained excellent benevolent gurus, and have the power to discriminate between those actions to be practised and those to be abandoned. At such a time, you should certainly take advantage of the opportunity presented by this fully-endowed human form. Doing this, however, depends on one thing only: becoming involved in the teachings of the Buddhas. But you have not done this perfectly merely by being a kind person. Either you yourself must know, without any doubt in your mind, through the proper stages for entering the teachings, or you have to depend on someone else who knows how to lead you through them.

To think that the great scriptural texts are meant to be merely dry, scholarly expositions of the Dharma, and that even the smallest teachings explained in the oral tradition are meant to be profound subjects for meditation, in other words to think of these two as being exclusive in purpose, is to miss the point of the teachings altogether. It is like what is always recited from the *Mahayanasutralamkara* by Maitreya about the scriptural teachings of Buddha and their Indian commentaries, the Kagyur and Tangyur, as well as about the oral traditions based on them: 'They lend themselves to being subjects for learning, debating and practising for the attainment of Buddhahood.' Thus, by saying they lend themselves to the practice of the attainment of Buddhahood, it means that their only purpose is to lead you to practise the teachings.

However, not just any teacher will do. He must be an able teacher who knows the nature of the path, its specific and graduated stages. He must be like this, because if he mistakes the wrong path for the right one, or the right for the wrong one, you will be misled even though you practise the Dharma exactly as he teaches it. Like a wrongly-prescribed medicine, it would do you nothing but harm. In addition, even though he may know the nature of the path well, if he deletes any of the important stages from it, or adds any unnecessary ones to it, his teachings will also not be effective. Thus, by not knowing for certain the specific path, and, in particular, by proceeding while omitting certain essential points and sidetracking onto the superfluous practice of unnecessary ones, he will be leading you astray.

In addition, even though he may know for certain the nature of the specific path, if he does not know how to apply the teachings to the development of your mind by leading you along stage by stage from the beginning to the end, then he will be acting as follows. Suppose he thought that this were a medicine. In particular, suppose he thought that it would be appropriate to prescribe it to a patient for his sickness simply because it was a good one. If he did actually prescribe it, thinking it to be the best and most powerful medicine, not only might it not help his patient, but it might in fact cause him great harm and even kill him. Likewise, suppose he thought these tantric teachings were the pure Dharma. In particular, suppose he thought that since tantra was the most profound Dharma, what wrong could there possibly be in teaching it? If he did actually lead you by means of it, he would benefit you only if he were to follow the proper graduated path in teaching it. If he did not follow this path, then not only would he not benefit you, but he might actually cause you to lose your chance of attaining your goal. This would be a rebirth in one of the three fortunate states if you were a person of initial-level motivation, liberation if of intermediate level or the full enlightenment of Buddhahood if you were a person of advanced-level motivation. Therefore, it is most important for him to know the proper graduated path of the teachings.

Furthermore, although he may know the importance of teaching in this way, he himself must have gained certainty about the stages in the path by being led in great detail by a learned teacher in a very thorough study of the many great scriptural texts of the standard authors. For the main abbreviated points of the oral tradition explanations, which show disciples the way along the graded path without faltering, are all derived from and are based on these great scriptural texts, which are difficult to understand in detail by themselves. This they do by presenting their main points in a logical abbreviated form suitable for teaching, but which out of necessity, however, violate the original textual order.

As for the proper gateway for entering the practice of the teachings, once you have found a qualified teacher as described above, consider the following quotations. Nagarjuna has written in his letter, the Suhrllekha, to the king of Andra, 'O you who are free from the fears of samsara, I am at a loss as to what more to say. But if you insist, here is a useful piece of advice: "Try to tame your mind!" As Buddha had said, "The mind is the root of the Dharma in that by means of it you can know which are the non-virtuous actions to be abandoned and which the virtuous actions to be practised."' Aryadeva has said in his *Madhyamika-catuhsataka,* 'I see no gateway other than the mind for living beings to accumulate black or white karmic merit. For this reason, I shall first give a few words of explanation about the mind.' Thus, as the noble, fatherly Nagarjuna and his son-like disciple Aryadeva have both said, the root of all virtuous and non-virtuous actions is nothing but the mind. It is certain that there can only be three gateways for entering into the practice of virtuous actions and abandoning non-virtuous ones, namely the body, speech and mind. Know then that of these three, the body and speech are under the influence of the mind. Thus, you must concentrate on taming your mind as the proper gateway for practising the teachings.

To continue: firstly, it is very important to have the correct motivation for your practice, for it not to be mere words. No matter how much more I could say about the graduated order of correct motivation, the most common and helpful scheme for minds of all scopes and capacities, from small to great, is as follows. First, when you are at the stage of initial-level motivation, you must strive your hardest to produce the type of mind that seeks to benefit your future rebirths, by no longer being concerned with this life alone. This you should do by remembering death, as you will not be in this present body for ever. You should also meditate a great deal on how you can go to either of the two possible states of rebirth after this life: either to one of the three fortunate states of rebirth – as a god, anti-god or human; or to one of the three unfortunate states – as an animal, hungry ghost or hell creature. You should also meditate on how the causes for rebirth in these different realms depend on the white karma accumulated from virtuous actions and the black karma accumulated from non-virtuous ones.

Then, when you are at the stage of intermediate-level motivation, you must cultivate at length the type of mind that takes an ardent interest in liberation, by turning away from the lures of the cycle of samsara. This you should do by exerting great effort in thinking about the advantages of the peaceful state of liberation and the disadvantages of all states of rebirth in samsara.

Then, when you are at the stage of advanced-level motivation, you should try to develop your mind to the secure and stable state at which you can aspire to attain Buddhahood. This you should do by turning right away from all selfish thoughts concerned only with your own welfare. Such thoughts cause you to ignore the need to make others happy or to alleviate their suffering. But once you are concerned to help others, the best means to accomplish your goal is clearly nothing short of attaining Buddhahood yourself. This you should do by developing three good habits in particular. The first is love, wishing that all who are happy should remain so. The second is compassion, wishing that all who suffer should become liberated. And the third, bodhicitta, is the enlightened motive assuming the responsibility to work to attain Buddhahood yourself in order to be able to liberate all living beings from their suffering and to ensure their happiness. These will become habits once you have realized that just as you yourself feel good when happy, and terrible when suffering, so do all living beings.

However, your practice will not bring you insight if your motivation to know, ponder and meditate on the teachings of a certain practice intended to develop your mind is the intellectual curiosity aroused from a partial understanding of a few words of it. This motivation is, after all, rooted in the fundamental error of seeking ego-gratification and security in the mere amassing of knowledge, which is contradictory to that of the practice of developing your mind. Take myself, for example: I might say I am doing a certain practice for the sake of my future life, for liberation, or I might even say, with many sweet-sounding words, for the sake of liberating all living beings. But I find that the natural inclination of my mind is such that it works either for benefits for myself in this lifetime, or for what I might call liberation, but which in fact is only for a few of the fruits of happiness to be had in samsara. Intellectually, however, I understand that all this is nothing but a selfish aim directed today at one thing, tomorrow at something else, and which is an incorrect motivation for successful practice.

Therefore, in order to develop your mind successfully, without having to force or fake it, a mere intellectual understanding of the meaning of all the teachings concerning the development of your mind is not enough. You must also meditate beforehand to confirm your motivation by becoming fully convinced of the validity of the practice and the worth of attaining its goal. As for the method of this preliminary meditation, you should develop the habit of practising over and over again what is called examination meditation. This is the type of meditation done prior to any formal practice. In it you examine with the four types of logic all the factors proving the validity of the practice and the worth of attaining its goal. Thus, you should test the teachings to see if they are internally consistent, if they make empirical sense from your past experience, if they satisfactorily explain anything you can think of, and if their practice actually does work to produce their stated goals from the examples of the fully realized high Gurus you have met who have mastered them.

Thus, in whatever practice you use to develop your mind, the main factor leading to successful insight is your preliminary examination meditation. In it you focus on the reasons for aiming at the goal of the practice – in other words, why you want to become enlightened – and on the detailed aspects of the purpose the goal is to be put to once attained: in other words, what you are going to do once you have become enlightened. But this is not enough in itself. Between meditation sessions you must confirm for yourself that you know what the teachings say, so that you have a store of sound knowledge on which to have insights. This certainty is gained from reading scriptural texts and their perfect commentaries, together with hearing oral explanations relating to the subject of your practice.

In addition, you must also eliminate the possibility of any

detrimental factors, physical or mental, arising that prevent you from doing your practice as a result of your previously acquired black karma. Moreover, you must also build up the contributory supporting factors which will form a store of meritorious experiences on which to build insight. Both of these come from the prerequisite practice of what is called collecting and cleansing, or the 'preliminaries.' This consists of two parts. One is the cleansing of the black karmic consequences of your previous non-virtuous actions through the admission that you had acted incorrectly and through the repeated invocation of the four opponent powers. These four are as follows. Firstly, you must summon before you mental images of the Three Jewels of Refuge: Buddha, Dharma, and Sangha. As these are the actual objects against which you have committed your non-virtuous actions, you must take refuge in them and offer them your bodhicitta vow to practise for the attainment of Buddhahood in order to be able to liberate all living beings from samsara. Then you must offer the merit of whatever virtuous actions you are doing, such as making religious offerings and prayers, towards the liberation of all living beings. Then, remembering the non-virtuous actions you have committed, you must feel sincere regret for them, not guilt. Finally, you must offer your promise to turn away from all such non-virtuous actions in the future. In this way, the obstacles that might arise as a result of these non-virtuous actions can be avoided.

The other part of the collecting and cleansing practice is the collection of a store of good merit to replace your previous store of black karma. This is built up from the experience of making at least one hundred thousand prostrations, mandala offerings, repetitions of the hundred-syllable mantra of Vajrasattva, and the mantra of your Guru's Sanskirt name, and from offering all the merit from this for the sake of the liberation of all living beings. All these must be done sincerely and conscientiously, bearing clearly in mind what you are doing and why, so as not to fall into a mechanical practice or to mistake this as a penance to be done out of guilt.

In this way you will amass each and every one of the contributory factors of building up stores of sound knowledge and meritorious experience, and of eliminating your previous store of black karma. Together, these will provide the underlying basis for achieving successful insights into whatever practice you take up to develop your mind, namely the clarification of both the goal of the practice and the purpose of achieving it. This is done in examination meditation when, with the wisdom that understands all the particulars, you weigh very carefully the advantages of following the practice and the disadvantages of not. Therefore, once you have finished amassing these contributory factors as above and have done the examination meditation, you can be confident that the practice will work to bring you special insights for developing your mind. Thus, by doing all this, you can have confidence that you will gain successful insights into the very smallest part of your experience of whatever you practise.

To summarize, it is necessary to have confidence that you will gain successful insights into whatever practice you take up to develop your mind. This you achieve by being convinced beforehand that certain special results will follow from the practice once you have blocked off the possibility of any obstacles arising as a result of your previous store of black karma and have built up the contributory factors that will aid your practice, namely stores of sound knowledge and meritorious experiences. If you realize that doing only this much is not enough, you will not make the mistake of abandoning any of the teachings of the pure Dharma. This you would do if you thought that once you had done this much, then everything else would follow automatically and you would not have to do anything further.

Therefore, granted that this preliminary state of mind, confident of what it is aiming at and why, is what you must develop first, you must remember that it is not enough

merely to have developed it. You must sustain it throughout your practice. Not only must you sustain it, however;
you must really try to increase it as much as possible. This
is because some people mistakenly think that this examination and confirmation of motivation is only a preliminary
practice and that it is unnecessary to continue it as a habit.
Others mistakenly think that it is not really necessary to be
continually concerned about their motivation decreasing,
because they believe that merely having done this preliminary practice once is sufficient to guarantee it for the rest of
their practice. On the other hand, there are still others who
mistakenly think that these ideas about proper motivation
involve practices that are not really the heart of the matter,
and, like the husk or the outer shell, it is all right to forget
about them. So, disregarding them, they pay attention only
to the actual meditation itself. But if you hold any of these
mistaken beliefs, then you have never really understood the
point of following the path of the Dharma at all. Because, if
you meditate as your way of practising the Dharma and lack
the proper motivation for so doing, as explained above, and
especially if you do this meditation devoid of the
enlightened motive of bodhicitta, then your practice will
only be an imitation of the real thing. Even if you do pure
meditation on shunyata with single-minded concentration,
you cannot possibly be considered a Mahayana Buddhist.
This is because you lack bodhicitta as your motivation, and
the importance of bodhicitta has been stressed by Buddha
more than once.

Therefore, Buddha, who knows all the most effective
means for living beings to attain their goals, has taught two
very wise methods, both to cause the beneficial merit accru-
ing during your actual meditation sessions to go towards
the right aim, namely your attainment of Buddhahood, as
well as to keep this merit from decreasing. These two are to
meditate on bodhicitta at the beginning of each meditation
session, and at its conclusion to steer, with great waves of
prayer, the beneficial merit of the meditation towards your

attainment of Buddhahood. Thus it is not enough to pray for just anything. You should be very certain to reach the heart of all prayer by praying conscientiously for your attainment of Buddhahood in order to be able to liberate all living beings from samsara.

Then, when you practise the meditations on the two stages of the tantric path, you should cherish doing so on the foundation of developing your mind to such a state, in such a way, for such a purpose, and holding on to the determination never to let it weaken.

2 Tantra

In general, whenever you enter the door of any of Buddha's vehicles, either to liberation or enlightenment, you must set the foundation for your success by your own pure discipline of moral self-control. This you should do by keeping purely either the five ordination vows of a lay-person, the thirty-six of a novice monk or nun, the two hundred and fifty-three of a fully ordained monk, or the three hundred and sixty-four of a fully ordained nun. But, in particular for entering the secret vehicle of tantra, in addition to maintaining your discipline of moral self-control, it is very important to secure your bodhicitta motivation which, as I have explained above, is the ultimate essence of the entire Mahayana path.

Then, when you have received a proper formal initiation from a fully qualified tantric master, do not forsake your complete set of sixty-four bodhicitta vows and twenty-two tantric vows, both the root and minor ones, which you had given your sacred word of honour to keep. Breaking any of the eighteen root bodhicitta vows or any of the fourteen root tantric vows would cause you to completely lose the effective empowering of the initiation. Moreover, it is very good not to break any of the minor vows which, while not completely destroying the empowerment, would certainly cause it to weaken. Otherwise, if you do cause yourself to lose it, you must retake all the vows and once more give your sacred word of honour to keep them by receiving another initiation. This you must do in order to eliminate completely the detrimental consequences of having broken your previous set of vows, and to be able to start off again with a clean slate. Therefore, having recognized precisely what the consequences are of breaking the root and minor vows, you should discipline yourself never to break them again once you have received the initiation, taken the vows and given your sacred word of honour a second time.

However, you should try from the very beginning never to become stained by breaking any of the root vows. Moreover, if you should happen to break any of the minor vows, you should cleanse yourself of the consequences of this which would weaken the effective empowering of the initiation. This can be done by means of the purification ceremony in which you admit you have acted incorrectly, invoke the four opponent powers, and offer the purification prayer.

Therefore, as I see it, receiving a proper initiation and keeping your vows and sacred word of honour pure are the foundation for the meditations on the two stages of the tantric path. Without these, you cannot possibly succeed in their practice. As you must at least keep your vows and sacred word of honour if you receive an initiation but do not actually practise the meditations on the two stages of the tantric path, you must understand perfectly clearly the extreme importance of these procedures.

If you do keep your vows and sacred word of honour after receiving an initiation, then even if you do not actually practise the meditations on the two stages of the tantric path during this lifetime, Buddha has said that you will attain the highest goal of Buddhahood in no less than seven and no more than sixteen rebirths. On the other hand, suppose you do the meditations on the two stages of the tantric path, but treat lightly the vows which you have given your sacred word of honour and promised to keep. In this case, Buddha has said that not only will you fail to attain the highest goal of Buddhahood, but you will also fall to one of the three unfortunate states of rebirth as well.

Buddha has said that if you are practising tantra as a lay-person, you must still keep the five lay ordination vows, and, if as a member of the monastic order, either the two or three sets of vows, depending on whether you are a novice or a fully ordained monk or nun. Buddha has also said that for the practice of tantra it is best to be fully ordained, next best a novice, and at minimum a lay-person. The reason for this is not just because of the difference in the number of vows each of them promises to keep, but rather the difference in the number they actually keep pure. This is why Kamalashila in his *Madhyamikaloka* has said that if you practise tantra on the foundation of purely-kept ordination and bodhicitta vows, you will achieve results even more quickly. Thus, he is claiming that you will achieve results more quickly if you take tantric vows after you have already been keeping pure ordination and bodhicitta vows, than if you had only been keeping pure the tantric vows alone.

It is the same even if you are only practising the non-tantric Mahayana path of the perfections. There will be greater results if you take bodhicitta vows after ordination vows than if you take bodhicitta vows alone. This is what is meant when it is stated in many scriptural texts that if there were two bodhisattvas equal in all respects except that one was a lay-person and the other a monk or nun, the latter would be more praiseworthy.

It seems, however, that there are many people who can explain the specifics of the vows and so forth by merely listing them in words. But when it comes to putting them into practice, it seems there are very few who actually do keep them. This I find very difficult to understand.

But to continue: as is commonly taught, 'The Omniscient Buddha has shown the following method as the proper steps to follow for attaining Buddhahood. Once you have practised the development stage of tantra well, then and only then should you go on to practise the completion stage.' Thus, it is saying that just as you must climb the lower steps of a flight of stairs before you can possibly proceed to the higher ones, so likewise in order to proceed to Buddhahood, you must meditate on the development and completion stages of tantra, not in just any order, but properly.

You must meditate on the development stage first: Buddha has said that if you omit it your practice will not work. The practice of this development stage might not necessarily bring you special extra-sensory powers for worldly purposes, such as telepathy or clairvoyance, or rid you of such temporary unpleasant things as sickness or poverty. Nevertheless, the fact that following the practice of the development stage is an integral part of the path for attaining supreme Buddhahood has been well established and has sound scriptural support in many tantric texts. Therefore, you should do the practice of the development stage by meditating on a circular mandala that has been properly laid out by an expert tantric master.

In addition, for successful practice, you must have acquired beforehand the two accumulations of good merit and meditational insights, as explained above. Also, between meditation sessions, you must continually keep in mind the fact that you have taken on the form of the meditational deity who represents that aspect of full enlightenment of Buddhahood to which you are karmically attracted. Also, keep in mind that you are assuming this form in order to attain Buddhahood through it, to be able to liberate all living beings from their sufferings, and that your surroundings are the mandala abode of this meditational deity. In addition, you must recite the mantra of this aspect of Buddha, always imagining all your words as this mantra. Moreover, you should make offerings to yourself as this meditational deity, visualizing whatever you received as

190 The Geluk Tradition

being offered to him or her and whatever you give the deity as being offered to his or her protector and minor forms. While you are doing all this, you must make sure that your recitation of the syllables of the mantra and the words of the prayers accompanying the offerings are not merely mechanical. As it is necessary to impress on your mind both the words of what you are reciting as well as their meanings, why not take pleasure in so doing?

Then, as it is very important to know how to meditate with single-minded concentration that you have become the meditational deity during your actual meditation sessions, I shall say a few words of explanation about how to do this.

It will certainly be much easier for you to know how to practise this meditation if you know beforehand what scope of single-minded concentration you wish to develop once you have become accustomed to meditating on this development stage. Let us consider, therefore, an example of a certain scope of single-minded concentration you might wish to develop.

If you are meditating, for instance, with the wish to be able to visualize clearly the complete circle of the mandala with yourself in the form of the main meditational deity in the centre, all at once in one all-encompassing vision of single-minded concentration, you should do as follows. From the very beginning, start visualizing both the main central meditational deity as well as the mandala in which he resides, together with his body colour, what he holds in his hands, his adornments and clothing, as well as the specifics of the colours and shapes of the mandala. This you must try to do at once.

Therefore, as the first step you must train yourself to visualize just one facet of the complete visualization. If the facet you were going to train yourself to visualize first were, for instance, yourself as the main central meditational deity of this complete visualization, I would tell you to train yourself in the following manner.

Actually, there are two standard ways of doing this. One is to train yourself to build up a clear mental image of the meditational deity in progressively longer stages by visualizing first one specific fine detail of the body and then expanding from there. The second way is to start with a rough visualization of the entire form and then to fill in the details. Of these two methods, the former is only fit for a few special people. The latter, however, is more effective for the general practitioner and is easier to do.

Therefore, of the two aspects of the main central meditational deity, namely his rough form and his details, you must first visualize yourself as the complete deity, from his head to his feet, in his roughest form. When you can see this clearly, you must fix your attention on this and maintain it without letting your mind wander. If the total body is clear in your mind, then you should fix your attention on that. But if the total body becomes unclear and only a few parts of it are left, you should fix your attention on those parts that remain clear. If even these parts disappear from your mind, you must start again to visualize yourself as having the entire form and try to fix your attention on that once more. If while you are meditating something appears in your visualization and does not belong there, you should cast this out of your mind and return to fixing your attention on the original visualization.

For beginners it has been said that if meditation sessions on these visualizations are too long, they will not be effective at all. According to my own experience, I find that this is so. Therefore, if you try to have as many short sessions as possible, your development of single-minded concentration will proceed without fault.

Moreover, when you start you must keep your mind alert and try to maintain this clarity. If when meditating you do not keep alert and are unaware that your mind is becoming either dull or agitated, then you may waste a lot of time and achieve only a coarse understanding. Although you may spend an entire lifetime doing a muddled meditation like this, you will never develop single-minded concentration as you had wished. Therefore, please always watch out for this in your meditation.

In general, single-minded concentration, as for example in visualizing yourself as having the rough form of the main central meditational deity, has four defining characteristics which must all be present for it to be considered complete and proper. You must be able to visualize whether or not this requires a great deal of effort. You must maintain unbroken concentration on this visualization throughout the entire meditation session. While concentrating in this way you must not let your mind become either full or agitated. And, in the end, you must experience the exhilarating feeling of physical ecstasy and mental bliss caused by being able to focus and use your concentration at will. All these defining characteristics are held in common with the single-minded concentration developed in the mental quiescence meditation practised on the Sutrayana path as well. The main difference, however, is that in this latter type of meditation you visualize Buddha or other meditational deities before you, rather than yourself as actually having taken on these forms, as in Tantrayana practice.

Then, not only must your concentration on yourself as having the rough form of the main meditational deity be firm, but you must also pay careful attention to all the details as well. Then when you expand the scope of your concentration to include around you the minor deities in the visualization mandala, you must not lose the clarity of your visualization of yourself as the main deity. You must visualize all of this together at one time with the same degree of clarity throughout. If you ignore the main central figure and merely focus on the other minor forms, how will you ever be able to concentrate on the entire visualization all at once?

Thus, the development stage as explained like this is a subject without which the noble tantric texts would be incomplete. As it is extremely important and extensively praised as being a very valuable part of the tantric path, it is essential that you practise these meditations on the development stage.

The completion stage of tantra was known to the earlier teachers as having two parts: the non-profound and the profound completion stage. As for the former, they believed it to be a meditation on such things as energy channels, energy-wind and seminal fluid. If you wish to study only this, however, you should search out their teachings on this subject yourself. They believed that the latter of these was a meditation on shunyata (emptiness). Granted that both these types of meditation are to be practised on the completion stage, you should examine this point yourself to see whether or not they form two separate parts of the completion stage.

3 *Emptiness*

It is taught that the insight of shunyata (emptiness) is of equal importance for both the Sutrayana and Tantrayana paths, for the great masters have commented that this is so. The methods for the development of single-minded concentration on shunyata, however, which are less known in the Sutrayana teachings are found in more abundance in the Tantrayana. But, although the Tantrayana is distinguished in that it is easier to realize shunyata through it, there is nothing better than the Sutrayana teachings as a method for gaining a proper intellectual understanding of shunyata first. This is made clear by the many quotations and logical arguments found in the sutras. Therefore you should really try to settle on an intellectual understanding of shunyata first by becoming acquainted with and thinking about the meaning of what is taught in the Sutrayana texts and commentaries, specifically those that discuss the profound meaning of shunyata, until you understand them. Discard all misleading teachings that diverge and lead you away from the true meaning of shunyata. It is improper to follow these. The texts you should study in order to become certain of shunyata's real meaning are, for instance, the six logic texts of Nagarjuna.

It seems that there are a few very special people who, while not having studied very long in this lifetime, may have an instinctive understanding of the profound meaning of shunyata. But such instances are extremely rare. As for everyone else, they must search for their understanding of shunyata by examining the two standard lines of reasoning. First, nothing has true independent self-existence as an individual whole, because everything is made of parts. If something had true independent self-existence, it would not be dependent upon its parts. Second, nothing has true independent self-existence as a group consisting of many individuals. This is because none of the component individual parts has true indpendent self-existence according to the first line of reasoning.

However, you might assert that there is another easier line of reasoning than this for gaining a quicker understanding of shunyata. For instance, you may believe that by realizing that one particular thing has no true independent self-existence, you have automatically cut off your belief in general that all things have such self-existence. The learned masters would not be pleased with this incorrect line of reasoning. Therefore, when you search for an understanding of shunyata by studying the Sutrayana texts and logic, you should be aware that there can always be two ways of developing an understanding of it: either a correct or an incorrect way.

As for the incorrect way, this would be as follows. Suppose you were examining with the many kinds of logical reasoning the true, independent, self-existence of the development of things and their termination. You might falsely conclude that all distinction among things on the relative level of truth are invalid. Consequently, you would find nothing left by which to recognize anything. Because of this you would incorrectly think of samsara as being like a barren woman incapable of conceiving. You would then see all living beings when tied to samsara by karma and delusions as being paradoxically like children in the womb of this barren woman, and when freed of samsara as being delivered from this barren womb. You would see the sufferings that grow from non-virtuous actions as being no different from the horns that grow from a rabbit's head. Thus you would see all ordinary things on the relative level of truth as appearances exactly the same as images in a mirror, and you would say that all conceptions of these things were false precisely because these things were images and nothing more. In this way you would be dismissing all things on the relative level of truth and would be left with literally nothing at all.

From this incorrect understanding of the *Madhyamika*, or Middle Way teachings, there are two false conclusions you could further draw. One would be the assertion of the nihilist position. You would have found nothing left on the relative level of truth by which to recognize things and would dismiss all conceptions or understandings of things on this relative level of truth as being untrue. Because of this you might draw the false conclusion that shunyata, which asserts the lack of true, independent, self-existence of all things on the relative level of truth, was itself incorrect as well. In implying this, you would be denying the teachings of Buddha, which is a grave mistake indeed. It is possible by the power of the insight of shunyata to eliminate the black karmic consequences of even the obstacles from previously collected karma that are extremely difficult to overcome. But if you were to deny shunyata and thus abandon the teachings of the *Perfection of Wisdom (Prajnaparamita)*, you would be like the people described in the following quotation from the chapter called 'Hells' from the *Mahasmrtyupasthanasutra:* 'Whoever abandons shunyata is protector-less and goes to the Avici Hell of Uninterrupted Pain.' This means that once you have abandoned shunyata you are left with no other refuge to protect you, and thus you must remain for a long time in the lowest hell, called Avici.

The other false conclusion you could draw from this incorrect understanding of shunyata would be as follows.

You would have accepted shunyata on the ultimate level of truth but would see everything on the relative level as being mere mental conceptions to which your mind attaches a name and believes is real. Included would be such practices to train your mind as the vast teachings of the meditations on the development stage of tantra, the trainings to develop bodhicitta, taking refuge, and so forth, as well as all Dharma teachings you might hear or read and think about. Then you might further falsely conclude that mental conceptions are things that tie you to samsara. Thus you would ignore and despise all these actions bringing you good karmic effects, such as taking refuge, doing meditation, and so on. In so doing, you would be opening the door for you to fall into one of the three unfortunate stages of rebirth.

If you maintain either of these two mistaken positions it is the same in that in neither case do you have any true understanding of shunyata. Rather, all you have is the arrogance of feeling that you have attained everything when actually you have attained nothing at all. Of these two, the first position, which nihilistically denies even shunyata, is quite divorced from all respect and incentive that would cause you to take an interest in finding out what shunyata really means in the first place. The second position, which accepts shunyata only on the ultimate level of truth, allows for a partial respect and interest in shunyata and nothing more.

If your incentive for finding out the real meaning of shunyata is destroyed, even if you accept the theory of shunyata but have a wrong understanding of it, as in the above two mistaken positions, need I explain about those who angrily refuse to accept shunyata at all? As Nagarjuna has said in his *Ratnavali*: 'Consider those who have faith in something with a wrong understanding of it and those who despise something with close-minded hostility. If it is explained that even those with faith can destroy their incentive to search for a right understanding of what they believe in, is there any need to mention those who are hostile?'

Nagarjuna also said in the same work, 'If your understanding of shunyata is mistaken, it does not matter how educated you are. You are wasting your intelligence. And if you do not accept shunyata at all, then you are left stuck in this impure world of suffering. Moreover, if you maintain an incorrect view of shunyata, and if in your stupidity you feel arrogant about how clever you are for having figured out shunyata, then, in abandoning the correct view, not only does your egotism make you unsuitable for Buddhahood, but rather it causes you to land in Avici hell instead and to remain there, standing on your head.'

Concerning the correct way of understanding shunyata Nagarjuna has said in his *Bodhisattvapatheyashastra*: 'After understanding the nature of all things as being void of any true, independent, self-existence, if you can still prove the operative existence of karma and its effects, then that is really wonderful, that is really tremendous.'

Also, Matrceta Ashvaghosa has said in the *Varnanarhavarnanastotra*, 'You should never ignore the relative level of truth because of shunyata. Rather, you should understand that the relative level of truth and shunyata on the ultimate level work in harmony with each other.'

Thus, as has been said, there are two realizations that you must come to in order to reach a proper and correct understanding of shunyata. The first comes when you search for an object that has true, independent, self-existence from the point of view of the ultimate level of truth. No matter what you look at, you cannot find one single atom which has such existence. The second follows in consequence of the first realization. It is that you become fully convinced because of this of the operative existence, from the point of view of the relative level of truth, of such things as cause and effect, the ways in which delusions bind you to samsara and how to eliminate this, the ways in which beneficial results follow from virtuous actions, and so on. The acceptance of the first of these two realizations is in accordance with the standard position of the Madhyamika Prasangika School. In further accepting the second of these two as well, there is no need to feel uncomfortable. There is no need to make excuses about this, saying that this is the point of view of others or a mistaken point of view. This is because both these insights are seen to be correct and non-contradictory. If you could see this as well, that would be very wonderful. This is because if you can see how there are actually no contradictions in what people ordinarily conceive of as being contradictory, then by that understanding you have found an effective method of teaching them.

Therefore, in understanding shunyata, you should also recognize that the distinction on the relative level of truth between those things that bind you to samsara and those that liberate you from it is valid and correct. Although you may understand shunyata correctly on the ultimate level of truth, if you still cannot recognize any valid distinctions among things on the relative level, there is no difference between your understanding of shunyata and that of the Sarvastivadin School. The Sarvastivadins say that if you were to accept shunyata on the ultimate level of truth, then there would be no distinction between things on the relative level. But, as there obviously are distinctions between things on the relative level of truth, therefore there is no shunyata. The Sarvastivadins have thus never understood shunyata from the beginning.

Nagarjuna has answered the following objection in the *Madhyamikaprajnamula*, 'If everthing were ultimately void of any true independent self-existent nature, then there would be no creation and no destruction, and it would follow that there would not be even the four noble truths. How do you explain that? In answer to this objection that if everything were ultimately void of any true, independent, self-existent nature, then there would be no distinction between those things binding you to samsara and those liberating you from it, I would say it is precisely the reverse. Both creation and destruction are dependent functions, arising from their causes according to the law of dependent arising.

Therefore it is only if everything were not ultimately void of any true, independent, self-existent nature – in other words, it is only if things did have true, self-existence, independent of their causes – that it would follow logically that there would be no creation and no destruction of things and that there would not be even the four noble truths.' Thus, Nagarjuna has explained that it is wrong to maintain that everything has a true independent self-existent nature. Creation and destruction of things arise dependently from their causes. Only if things had true self-existent natures independent of their causes would it invalidate creation and destruction. On the other hand, it is correct to maintain that everything is void of any true independent self-existent nature, precisely because it is from the interdependency of all things by the law of dependent arising that the creation and destruction of things can come about, dependent on their causes.

Nagarjuna also said in the same work, 'If it were correct to say that an object had shunyata as its ultimate self-nature, then all other assertions about its characteristics on the operative level of relative truth would follow correctly from the law of dependent arising. However, if it were incorrect to say that an object had shunyata as its ultimate self-nature, then no other assertions could follow correctly.' Thus, Nagarjuna has explained very clearly that if shunyata were valid, then everything else would follow accordingly; and if shunyata were not valid, then the situation would be reversed.

Your understanding of shunyata might be such that you think that if you were to discard all considerations of space and time concerning an object then you would be left with the actual object itself divorced from any reference or context by which to recognize it. If you were to say that with just this much understanding you had found the true insight of shunyata then there would not be much point to all the masters having said that the insight of shunyata is very difficult to gain. Even people of dull wits who have not

trained their mind at all can gain this simple-minded understanding of shunyata. But this much understanding alone is
not enough.

What makes the understanding of shunyata so difficult is
the problem of holding the following two insights together
without finding any contradiction between them. The first
is the pacification and elimination of all ideas of the true
independent self-existence of things from the point of view
of the ultimate level of truth. The second is the ability to
accept the operative existence of everything from the point
of view of the illusion-like relative level of truth at all, such
as all the distinctions between those things binding you to
samsara and those liberating you from it. As both these
insights are mandatory, if you do not know precisely the
differentiation of these two levels of truth, then you do not
understand shunyata as taught by Buddha. If you do know
this, however, then you are not ignorant of what Buddha
intended. Moreover, it is said that you can only reach the
goal of the perfection of the full enlightenment of Buddhahood by collecting the two accumulations. These are of
merit from virtuous actions done on the relative level of
truth and of insight gained into the ultimate level.

Scriptural support for the above statements is found in
the following texts. In the *Madhyamikaprajnamula*, Nagarjuna has said, 'Whoever does not understand precisely the
differentiation of the two levels of truth has not understood
the essence of the profound teachings of Buddha, namely
shunyata.' In the *Satyadvayavibhanga* Jnanagarbha has said,
'Those who understand precisely the differentiation of the
two levels of truth are not ignorant of the words of Buddha.
By collecting the complete accumulations of both merit and
insight, they perfect everything for the full attainment of
Buddhahood.'

It is said that this understanding of shunyata was difficult
even for the direct disciples of Buddha when Shakyamuni
Buddha himself was alive. According to the *Ratnagunasamcayagatha,* 'The teaching of the Buddhas is profound and

difficult to see. No one has ever understood it and no one has ever attained its realization without the help of a Guru, extensive study and meditational practice. Therefore after Shakyamuni Buddha, who had always performed virtuous acts out of compassion, had attained full enlightenment, he was concerned about who among all living beings would be able to understand it.'

Nagarjuna has written in the *Ratnavali* the following explanation of this point from the *Ratnagunasamcayagatha*, as well as an explanation by example of how it is impossible to obtain a quick and easy understanding of shunyata. 'Although it is obvious that our body is coarse; yet we are attached to it and cannot realize that it is unclean, full of delusions and impure. Although we see our body all the time, we cannot accept this fact, let alone comprehend it. If this is the case, then without having correctly perceived the teachings of the Dharma, how can we possibly gain a quick and easy understanding of the profound theory of shunyata which is so subtle and obscure? Because this teaching is so profound, Buddha realized that it would be very difficult for living beings to acquire the wisdom with which to understand it. This is why, after attaining full enlightenment, Buddha at first turned away from teaching shunyata.

In general, it is very rare to find a teacher who can really teach and a disciple who can really learn. More specifically, it is very rare to find someone who can effectively teach how to develop single-minded concentration on shunyata and someone who will study this and actually put it into practice. Therefore it seems to me that this matter cannot be ignored or approached in an undisciplined fashion.

It is impossible to seek a pure understanding of shunyata through faultless hearing or reading of correct explanations and through pondering their meaning, if you do not develop pure single-minded concentration on shunyata. Further, if you do not first have an intellectual understanding of the shunyata nature of all things, how can you possibly have a correct object for effective meditation on shunyata.

Not only this, but you must also be sure to search for either an actual state of mental quiescence (samatha) or a single-minded concentration (samadhi) having the four defining characteristics explained above, which would be something similar to mental quiescence. When you have settled on one of these two, you should then try to achieve a single-minded concentration joining mental quiescence with penetrative insight (vipassana) into shunyata. Then you will be able to focus single-mindedly on the profound meaning of shunyata divorced from all belief in the true independent existence of things.

If you do not have a correct understanding of shunyata, as explained above, then although you might achieve single-minded concentration, you would be unable to focus it on the true meaning of shunyata divorced from all belief in the true independent self-existence of things. Thus you would merely have mental quiescence without any penetrative insight into shunyata. Likewise, although you may have an unmistaken understanding of shunyata, if you did not have solid, strict mental quiescence, your mind would wander from object to object. Then, no matter how much you might examine shunyata, since you would not have combined mental quiescence and penetrative insight, you would be unable to focus on the true meaning of shunyata. That is why most reliable scriptural texts stress the necessity of having both mental quiescence and penetrative insight.

As for the way to develop a correct understanding of shunyata by eliminating all wrong views, if I were to explain these too briefly, I fear that it would not satisfy you. Yet if I were to explain this in too elaborate detail, I might run the risk of becoming entangled in a mass of words. Therefore I will not write in such detail.

In general, no matter how much I tried in the past to explain the details of the graded course to enlightenment in letter form, I never believed this would be much help. This was because I had always felt that those who would receive such a letter would not put it into practice. This is why, no

matter how many letters I have received in the past from
people both lofty and humble, requesting me to explain this
course, I have never previously consented to write out such
an explanation for them in letter form. But you, my noble
teacher, are exceptional and are unlike the others. Because
you have strongly and specifically requested this of me in
your honourable letter, and because I also see other compel-
ling reasons for answering you, I have ignored such things
as extensive scriptural quotations, elaborate arguments
from logic and fine examinations of logical conclusions
from academic details, and can now respectfully submit this
letter to you as a brief explanation. When you examine this
letter carefully with the four types of logic again and again,
if you find what I have written to be lucid and correct, please
try to put it all into practice.

Countless years ago when you were the Master Translator Lodan Sherab, you went to India under considerable
hardship and devoted yourself to many able teachers. Whatever wonderful works you have translated and written by
means of your understanding of the whole essence of the
teachings of Buddha in accordance with their true meaning,
they have all helped to clear the darkness of ignorance from
Tibet. With the compassionate mind of cherishing others
more than yourself, when you were this Master Translator,
this Eye of the World, Lodan Sherab, you attained the full
enlightenment of Buddhahood. The banner of your famous
name still waves on among all living beings, as well as the
gods. In order to fulfil all your purposes and wishes, I,
Lozang Dragpa, who am a meditator favouring solitude
and quiet places, following the wise masters who have practised the Dharma to the rule in accordance with the meaning
of what they have heard and read from many faultless scriptures, have exerted great effort in writing this to you, Konchog Tsultrim. As your name signifies, you are always
respectful of the three jewels of refuge and keep the pure discipline of moral self-control. You are wise, your intelligence is vast and you exert great effort in keeping all the

vows. By the virtuous power of the merit received from writing this, may all living beings be able to understand the Dharma just as Buddha taught it, with true exposition. By practising accordingly, may they all be able to attain the bliss of Buddhahood.

You, whose mind is always calm and virtuous, and I are like Buddha's disciples, the close friends Shariputra and Maudgalyayana. I pray that whichever one of us receives the nectar of Buddhahood first will be able to share it with the other.

Ah, isn't it wonderful to have had the good fortune to attain a human form fully endowed with the time and opportunity for Dharma study and for meeting with the teaching of Buddha's Dharma. Now we should make our fully-endowed bodies, through which we can achieve the highest goals, fit for practising the Dharma day and night. Buddha has said that those who strive with little effort gain little result, and those who strive with full effort gain full results. What intelligent person would be satisfied with only partial results?

In the past no single living being has escaped being consumed by the cannibal of the impermanence of death. As this still holds true, we should never relax our minds. We must stop involving ourselves in meaningless worldly activities which, although we may exert a great deal of effort on, we will have to abandon in the end when we die. Instead, we should always think of the effects of the black and white karma of our virtuous and non-virtuous actions, which, like our shadows, follow us wherever we go. Thinking this, we must try hard to tame our minds – a very hard task indeed. This we must do with firm humility, consideration of others, memory, alertness and care in performing virtuous actions. Having done all this, may we be able to die with peace of mind and no regrets.

May Buddha's Dharma, the basis of all happiness, flourish for a long time. May no harm come to those who practise the Dharma. May the hopes of all living beings be fulfilled in accordance with the Dharma. May the mutual love between us and between all living beings never be broken.

This concludes 'A Brief Exposition of the Main Points of the Graded Sutra and Tantra Courses to Enlightenment.' It has been written by the Buddhist monk, Lozang Dragpa, known as Je Tsongkhapa, at the Reura Monastery in east Tibet. It was in answer to a letter from Konchog Tsultrim, a noble teacher and leader of people, a worthy friend of the Dharma, and a great meditator who practises in accordance with the meaning of the many teachings he has heard and read.

Part Six
The Sakya Tradition

The Parting from the Four Attachments
Ngorchen Kunga Zangpo

*It is not worth being attached to this life since it is
like a bubble of water: the time of death is
uncertain. The three realms of existence are like
poisonous fruits. Though at present delicious,
they are accompanied by future harm; whoever is
attached to them is surely deluded. If one is
attached to one's own purpose, it is like cherishing
the son of an enemy. In the end it will certainly
bring harm. If one is attached to substantiality and
characteristics, it is like grasping for water in a
mirage. Although there is for the moment an
appearance of water, there is nothing to be drunk.*

Sakya Pandita

Introduction to Part Six

The teaching on *The Parting from the Four Attachments* is the basic mind-training method used in the Sakya tradition. When the Sakya Master Sachen Kunga Nyingpo (1092–1156) was only twelve years old he saw a vision of the Bodhisattva Manjushri and received these teachings directly from him. The four attachments are: (1) attachment to this life, which prevents one from being a religious person; (2) attachment to samsara, which prevents renunciation; (3) attachment to one's own purpose, which prevents the mind of enlightenment; and 4) grasping at the true existence of phenomena, which prevents a correct vision of reality.

The text given here is a manual of instruction on the original teaching of *The Parting from the Four Attachments*. It was taught by the fifteenth-century Sakya master Ngorchen Kunga Zangpo and transcribed by a monk called Kunga Lekrin. The quotations from the sutras that appear throughout the text were added later by another famous master, Jamyang Khyentse Wangpo.

The manual is in fact a step-by-step guide for contemplation. Each part is carefully outlined in a number of sections. The purpose of this kind of presentation is to assist the practitioner to reflect regularly and systematically on the methods of overcoming these four attachments. *The Parting from the Four Attachments* is regarded as a summary of the entire path to enlightenment. The practice of freeing oneself from each of the four attachments is also a means of realizing the corresponding four themes of Gampopa. Freeing oneself from attachment to this life is the means of accomplishing the first theme, that of turning the mind to the Dharma; freeing oneself of attachment to samsara is the means of accomplishing the second theme, that of practising the Dharma as a path, and so on.

The text was translated into English by His Holiness Sakya Trizin, the present head of the Sakya tradition, and Ngawang Samten Chophel. It was first published as part of a booklet entitled *A Collection of Instructions on the Parting from the Four Attachments*, in 1982.

Introduction and Preliminaries

With respect, I prostrate to the Guru and to Manjushri.

For the sake of all living beings, you must attain to the stage of Buddhahood; for that purpose you must listen to the profound, holy teaching and decide to practise its meaning. Possessing entirely the right attitude for listening to the Dharma, such as having produced the supreme enlightenment thought, you should request the teaching and then listen carefully.

The teaching presented here is the *Parting From The Four Attachments*, which is the only path of all the Tathagatas of the three times, and the essence of the practice of all the sutras, the profound speech of the Buddhas. In order to practise this teaching, a history of the lineage of teachers is first given so as to create the right belief and to acknowledge its genuine origin, and then the actual instructions are given.

I. HISTORY OF THE TEACHING

When the Lord of Yogis, the great Sakyapa, Sachen Kunga Nyingpo was twelve years old, he relied on the compassionate Bari Lotsawa as his guru. When listening to the Dharma, Bari Lotsawa said, 'You are the only son of a great

Dharma practitioner, so you must study well. For this purpose you need wisdom, so you must first meditate on the holy Manjushri.' Having said that, he bestowed the initiation and oral transmission of Manjushri.

Accompanied by his guru, Sachen sat in meditation retreat in the old temple. At first, some signs of obstacles arose, but he was able to overcome these through the meditation, recitation and water protection practice of blue Acala. After six months of practising the Manjushri meditation, one day Sachen actually saw the holy Manjushri. He appeared, clearly seated on a jewelled throne, his hands placed in the gesture of teaching, and with two attendant bodhisattvas. At that time Manjushri himself said,

> If you have attachment to this life,
>   you are not a religious person.
> If you have attachment to the world of existence,
>   you do not have renunciation.
> If you have attachment to your own purpose,
>   you do not have the enlightenment thought.
> If grasping arises, you do not have the view.

Thus he recited these four lines.

Later, as Sachen pondered the significance of these words, he realized that the entire training of all the sutras spoken by the Buddha was summed up here. Having seen this to be a profound teaching, he then put it into practice, and through this he obtained an insight into the knowledge of all dharmas.

This teaching was then bestowed by Sachen on his son, the precious master Sonam Tsemo. From him the teaching was passed on to the following lineage: Jetsun Rinpoche Dagpa Gyaltshen, Choje Sakya Pandita, Drogon Chogyal Phagpa, Zhang Konchog Pal, Tak Phugpa, Choge Sonam Gyaltsen Pal Zangpo, Lama Palden Tsultrim, Choge Yeshe Gyaltsen Pal Zangpo, and the holy guru Kunga Zangpo.

II. THE ACTUAL INSTRUCTIONS

The second part – the actual instructions – consists of the preliminary, the fundamental teaching, and the conclusion.

A. THE PRELIMINARY

1. *Taking Refuge*

The preliminary is divided into the taking of refuge and the creation of the enlightenment thought.

There are four main differences when taking refuge in the Mahayana tradition (as opposed to the Hinayana tradition). The first is the object in whom we take refuge. We take refuge in the precious Buddha, the Enlightened One, whose qualities are unimaginable, who possesses no faults whatsoever, and who is matchless among all living beings. We take refuge in the precious teaching, all the teachings and realizations which have been implanted on the minds of the Buddhas and irreversible bodhisattvas. We take refuge in the precious community [sangha], the irreversible bodhisattvas who practise in accordance with the proper behaviour and understanding. The second is the length of time for which we take refuge. The third is the person who takes refuge. It is not yourself alone, but, led by your parents, it is all sentient beings equal in number of space who take refuge. The fourth is the purpose of taking refuge. You take refuge with the wish to gain the stage of full and perfect enlightenment for the sake of all sentient beings. Keeping in mind the meaning of these words and with an undistracted mind, you should recite the following verses of refuge.

> I and all other sentient beings who are equal to the ends of space and who have been my previous mothers, from this time until the essence of enlightenment is reached, take refuge in the pre-

cious Buddha who is the guru; we take refuge in the holy Dharma which possesses the teachings and realizations; we take refuge in the holy sangha who are the children of the victorious ones.

Recite this as many times as possible. To conclude, you should recite the following prayer.

May the precious Triple Gem bless my mind to proceed towards the Dharma, bless me to traverse the path of the Dharma; bless me to dispel errors on the path; bless me that the illusive vision may appear as primordial wisdom; bless me that non-religious thoughts may never be produced even for a moment; bless me to obtain Buddhahood quickly.

2. *Creation of the Enlightenment Thought*

Next you should produce the enlightenment thought by reciting the following verses:

In Buddha, Dharma and the most excellent community I take refuge until enlightenment is reached. Through deeds of giving and the like, may I obtain Buddhahood for the sake of all living beings. I must obtain Buddhahood for the sake of all sentient beings, and for that purpose I will diligently accomplish virtuous deeds of body, voice and mind.

B. THE FUNDAMENTAL TEACHING

Second is the fundamental teaching of this text which is divided into four parts (in accordance with the parting from each of the four attachments).

1 *If You Have Attachment to this Life, You Are Not a Religious Person*

In order to practise the first subject of meditation, you should place your body either in the vajra position or in whatever posture you find comfortable, and then proceed with the recitation of the prayers of refuge and creation of the enlightenment thought. The first line, 'If you have attachment to this life, you are not a religious person,' means that you should not have attachment to this life. Though you may have attachment to the water of a mirage it will not quench your thirst, and it is the same with attachment to this life. If you have attachment to this life, then whatever moral conduct, hearing, contemplation and meditation you may perform will only culminate in the accomplishment of this present life's prosperity. It will not become an actual or proper Dharma practice. Therefore, as the master Vasubandhu said in his *Abhidharmakosa*.

> By possessing hearing and contemplation which are based on moral conduct, you should thoroughly apply yourself to meditation.

Thus, firmly based on the foundation of pure moral conduct you must first listen to the Dharma. Then you must contemplate its meaning to dispel doubts. Next, the meaning of that to which you listened and any doubts which are dispelled through contemplation should be meditated upon.

In order to produce a mind which desires to practise Dharma, you must meditate on the difficulty of obtaining the eighteen prerequisites needed for the proper practice of Dharma. In order to produce the supreme effort needed for the practice of Dharma, you must meditate on death and impermanence.

1. *The Difficulty of Obtaining the Prerequesites*

First, concerning the difficulty of obtaining the eighteen prerequisites, the master Shantideva said in his *Bodhicaryavatara,*

> This opportunity [of possessing the eighteen prerequisites] is extremely difficult to obtain. Having obtained this, you must accomplish the purpose of others. If benefit is not accomplished, it will be difficult to gain this opportunity in the future.

As Shantideva said, this vessel of the human body complete with all the prerequisites which are needed for the accomplishment of the holy Dharma is very difficult to obtain. Once we have obtained it, we must practise Dharma perfectly. We must meditate on this fact again and again.

To explain this in a little more detail, four aspects are to be considered: the difficulty of obtaining the prerequisites from the point of view of cause, the difficulty of obtaining them from the point of view of number, the difficulty of obtaining them from the point of view of example, and the difficulty of obtaining them from the point of view of nature.

First, the cause of obtaining this perfect vessel endowed

with the prerequisites is the necessity to perform virtuous deeds, such as moral conduct, and to abandon all non-virtuous activities. However, since the number of living beings in the three realms of existence who perform virtuous acts is few and the number who perform non-virtuous acts is very great, you must meditate on the idea of the difficulty of obtaining the prerequisites from the point of view of cause.

Second, when looking upon the sentient beings in this world, you see the number in the hells as being as great as the dust particles of this earth; the number of hungry ghosts as being as great as the snowflakes tossed about in a snowstorm; and the number of animals as being as great as the fermented grains in a vat of beer. In comparison with these, the number of those who have obtained the perfect human body is very small. So, you should meditate on the idea of the difficulty of obtaining the prerequisites from the point of view of number.

Third, as it says in the *Bodhicaryavatara,*

> Therefore the Blessed One said that it is much more difficult to obtain a human birth than it is for a turtle to place its neck through a hole in a yoke which is blown about in a great ocean.

As it says, a blind turtle lives in a vast ocean, and once every one hundred years he rises to the surface. Floating on this ocean, tossed about by waves, is a golden yoke in which is a single hole. Just as it is almost impossible for that turtle to place its neck through the opening of that yoke so, although there are unimaginable types of sentient beings, still it is almost impossible to be born as a human being. You should therefore meditate on the idea of the difficulty of obtaining the prerequisites from the point of view of example.

Fourth, to be free from the eight unfavourable places, such as birth as a fool or barbarian, and the acquisition of the ten favourable conditions is very rare. Therefore, you should meditate on the idea of the difficulty of obtaining the prerequisites from the point of view of nature.

Now, to explain these prerequisites in a little more detail. The eight unfavourable conditions which must be avoided are being born as a hell-being, a hungry ghost, an animal, a long-lived god, a barbarian, a person with wrong beliefs, a person born in a place to which a Buddha has not come, and a fool. The ten obtainments consist of five which are acquired by oneself and five which are acquired through others. The five self-obtainments are: to be born as a human being, to be in a central realm (where there are monks, nuns or lay people), to have sound organs, not to have committed the five heinous crimes (or even ordered others to perform such acts or rejoiced in their enactment by others), and to have faith in one's heart in the teachings on moral conduct of the Dharma. The five other obtainments are: a Buddha has come into the world, He taught the Dharma, the teaching has been maintained, there are followers of that teaching, and there are kind donors. Thus, the difficulty of obtaining the human body endowed with the eighteen prerequisites needed for the practice of Dharma should be explained in accordance with one's own and others' intelligence.

2. *Death and Impermanence*

Next, you should think about death and impermanence. As the master Sura said in his *Removing of Sorrow,*

> Death dwells in front of all that is born.

This is explained to mean that the conclusion of birth is certainly death. Therefore, you should meditate on the idea that, since you are going to die, you must practise Dharma quickly.

Now, to explain in a little more detail, this section is divided into three parts: to contemplate the certainty of death, to contemplate the uncertainty of the time of death, and to contemplate that only Dharma will benefit you at the time of death.

First, since all compounded phenomena are by nature impermanent, they are certain to be eventually destroyed. In the *Lalitavistara Sutra* it says,

> The three worlds are impermanent like autumn clouds: the birth and death of living beings is similar to viewing a dance; life is gone like a flash of lightning in the sky, quickly passing like a mountain waterfall.

Especially, as the master Sura said,

> If even the vajra-body, the rupakaya of the Buddhas, adorned with the major and minor marks of perfection, is impermanent, then our body which is like a bubble is by all means impermanent.

Thus it is said that even though the fully Enlightened One obtained the stage of immortality, still He showed the manner of entering into Parinirvana. So, ordinary persons like ourselves are certain to die. You must think about this idea.

Again, the master Sura said,

> Though a great sage may possess the five supernatural perceptions and fly unobstructedly in the sky, still he cannot go to a place where he enjoys immortality.

This means that wherever you go within the three realms of existence, you cannot find anywhere where you will not die. Therefore, you must meditate on the idea that you will certainly die.

From the fact that there are many causes of death but few causes of life, it is certain that you will die. Master Nagarjuna said in his *Ratnavali,*

> There are many causes of death and very few causes of life. Since those also can become the causes of death, you must always practise Dharma.

As he said, the causes of life, such as the place where you desire to live, your food, wealth, etc. can also become the causes of death. So you must meditate on the idea of the certainty of death.

Second, to contemplate the uncertainty of the time of death. As we can clearly see, the time of death is uncertain since some die inside the womb, some die at the time of birth, some die in old age, some die in youth, while some die in middle age. Therefore you must think about and meditate on the manner in which the time of death is uncertain.

Third, to contemplate that Dharma alone can benefit you at the time of death. No matter who you may be, whether an eloquent speaker, a powerful person, a person with many attendants and much wealth, or a brave person, and so on, you cannot turn death away, but must certainly die. At the time of death, nothing besides Dharma can help. Therefore, by practising Dharma for as long as you are alive, you will not feel regret at the time of death. You will be happy since you will be confident of being born in a good place. So you must certainly practise the holy Dharma. Since the time of death is uncertain, you must meditate on the idea of the need to practise Dharma immediately.

2 If You Have Attachment to the World of Existence, You Do Not Have Renunciation

This means that if you have attachment to the world of existence consisting of its three realms, then even though you may practise Dharma it will not lead you to the path of enlightenment. Therefore you must become non-attached to the world of existence. In order to accomplish this, through an explanation of the faults of the world of existence you will see that all the world of existence is of the nature of suffering. Because of this you will wish to abandon the world of existence and there will arise within your mind the search for liberation. Therefore, for the sake of producing the realization of this thought of renunciation, the faults of the world of existence are explained and the law of karma which causes you to be born in samsara is considered. Since you are ignorant of which deeds to perform and which to reject, you may carelessly indulge in non-virtuous actions. In order to know what is to be accepted and what is to be rejected in accordance with the law of cause and result (so that you may avoid suffering), the law of karma is taught.

1. *The Faults of the World of Existence*

In one sutra it is stated:

> The realm of desire is endowed with faults.
> Likewise, the realm of form is also endowed with
> faults. Also the formless realm is endowed with
> faults. It is only nirvana which is faultless.

As it says, no matter where you may be born within these
three realms, the place will be full of faults. This idea is
expanded on in the *Smrityupasthana Sutra,* where it is stated:

> The hell-beings experience the fire of hell; the
> hungry ghosts experience hunger and thirst; the
> animals experience the devouring of one another;
> humans experience short life; and the gods
> experience shamelessness. There is never any
> happiness on the needle-point of worldly exis-
> tence.

As it says, wherever you may be born among the six
types of living beings within the three realms of existence,
the place will be possessed of the nature of suffering. Since
whatever you partake of within this world is only the par-
taking of suffering, you must meditate on the thought of the
necessity of practising the pure Dharma which will lead you
to the path of enlightenment.

To explain further, we will consider the suffering of suffering, the suffering of change, and the suffering of the conditional nature of all things.

a. *The Suffering of Suffering*

The suffering of suffering consists of the suffering of the
hells, the suffering of hungry ghosts, and the suffering of
animals.

i. The Suffering of the Hells: There are three types of hell
which can be experienced: the suffering of the cold hells, the

suffering of the hot hells, and the suffering of the neighbouring and short-lived hells.

There are eight different cold hells. The first is called
'Blister Hell.' Here you take birth in a place where there is
no sun or shelter, which is surrounded by snow mountains,
and the inside of which is filled with ice. Because of an
incredibly cold wind, your entire body naturally turns to
blisters. The life span of one born there is described in the
Abhidharmakosha thus,

> The life span of the 'Blister Hell' is exhausted
> when a container of 1,600 kilograms of sesame
> seeds is emptied by removing one seed every one
> hundred years. The life spans of the other cold
> hells are twenty times the number of containers,
> in geometric progression.

Because of the increase in cold from the previous hell, the
second cold hell is called Bursting Blister Hell because
water, pus, blood and so on leak from the blisters on the
body. Third, because of an increase in cold from the previous hell, you suffer terribly. Since, as well as crying, you
make the sound 'brrrr,' it is called Brrrr Hell. Fourth,
because of an increase in cold from the previous one, you
suffer so that you are not even able to make a sound when
crying, only the sound of exhaling air, 'whisss.' So this is
called Whisss Hell. Fifth, because of a great increase in cold
from the previous hell, you do not have the power to say
anything at all. Your body is completely frozen, so this is
called Clenched Teeth Hell. Sixth, here it is much colder
than the previous hell and when an even stronger wind
blasts your body, your skin turns blue and cracks into eight
parts. This is therefore called Cracked Like an Utpala
Flower Hell. Seventh, because of the wind, the blue skin
breaks apart. The number of cracks therefore increases and
the body turns red, so it is called Cracked Like a Lotus Hell.
Eighth, because of even greater cold, your body is
thoroughly frozen inside and out so that you become like a

stone. Because the body cracks into sixteen parts, the intestines and entrails also crack into many pieces and this is called Cracked Like a Large Lotus Hell. You must keep in mind these sufferings and contemplate them again and again.

There are also eight hot hells. The first is called Reviving Hell. Because of the power of karma, you are born in a land consisting of burning iron. Your body is very youthful and you cling hard to your ego. Whatever you pick up automatically turns into a weapon. Whoever you see there is perceived to be your enemy, so that you cut and slash each other with your weapons. Your body is cut into many pieces, and you collapse into unconsciousness. Then, from the sky the sound 'revive,' is heard and a single cold wind touches your body. Thus your body again takes on a similar appearance to before, youthful, and so on. The second is called the Black Line Hell. Here the guardians of hell draw lines on your body, eight or sixteen, and so forth, and along these they cut you with saws and axes so that you experience countless sufferings. The third is called Crushing Hell. Here your youthful body is placed between mountains which look like the heads of goats and sheep and you are crushed between them so that you suffer terribly. The fourth is called Crying Hell. Here, on a burning iron ground, you are chased by the guardians of hell. Seeing a white house, you run to it and enter, thinking you will be able to escape there. The doors automatically close, and it becomes a burning iron house. You have no chance of escape from there. As the fire burns by itself you suffer terribly and cry out. The fifth is called Great Crying Hell. This hell has the same characteristics as the previous one, except that it has two houses (to escape from, rather than one). The sixth is called Hot Hell. Here the guardians of hell seize you and thrust a burning, one-pointed iron spear through your anus right up to the crown of your head, and thus you suffer. The seventh is called the Great Hot Hell. A three-pointed spear is thrust through your anus to the crown of your head. However, the right and left tips of the spear emerge through your right and left shoulders, and thus you suffer. The eighth is called Unceasing Hell (or, in Sanskrit, Avici Hell). Here, on a ground of burning iron the hell-being burns in such a way that you are unable to distinguish between the fire and the body of the one being burned. The only sign that gives you an idea that there is a hell-being there is the sound of his crying.

The length of the life span in these hells is described in the *Abhidharmakosha* as follows:

> Fifty human years are equivalent to one day in the life of the lowest of the six heavens of the realm of desire. In this manner, they live for five hundred years. The second heaven is twice as long as this. Understand that one day in the first hot hell, Reviving Hell, is equivalent to the life span of the lowest heaven, and that the next five hells are correspondingly as long as the next five heavens.

This means that fifty human years are equivalent to one day of life in the lowest heaven, Caturmaharaja kayika. Thirty of these days make one month, and twelve of these months make a year. A god in the Caturmaharaja kayika heaven lives for five hundred of these years. One day in Reviving Hell is calculated to be equivalent to this (that is, the life of a god in Caturmaharaja kayika heaven). Calculating in this way, the life span in Reviving Hell is five hundred of their own years. Similarly, one hundred human years are equivalent to one day of life in the second heaven, known as 'Thirty-three.' Life in this heaven lasts for one thousand of their own years, and this is equivalent to one day in Black Thread Hell. Calculating in this way, they live for one thousand of their own years. Two hundred human years are equivalent to one day in the heaven of Freedom From Fighting. Life in this heaven lasts for two thousand of their own years, and this is equivalent to one day in Crushing Hell. Calculating in this manner, they live for two thousand of their own years. Four hundred human years are equivalent to one day of life in the heaven of Joy. Life in this heaven lasts for four thousand of their own years, and this is equivalent to one day in the Crying Hell. Calculating in this way, they live for four thousand of their own years. Eight hundred human years are equivalent to one day in the heaven of Miraculous Joy. Life in this heaven lasts for eight thousand of their own years, and this is equivalent to one day in Great Crying Hell. Calculating in this manner, they live for eight thousand of their own years. One thousand, six hundred human years are equivalent to one day of life in the heaven Empowered by the Miracles of Others. Life in this heaven lasts for sixteen thousand of their own years, and this is equivalent to one day of life in Hot Hell. Calculating in this manner, they live for sixteen thousand of their own years. Life in Great Hot Hell lasts for half an intermediate aeon, and for a complete intermediate aeon in Unceasing Hell.

Furthermore, there are four types of neighbouring and short-lived hells. The first is called Fire-trench Hell, which is located at the perimeter of all the other hells. Whoever enters into this pit of fire has all his limbs burnt. When you lift up the right foot the burns are healed, but the left leg is burnt. Then, when the left leg is lifted up it is healed, but the right is burnt again. All of your internal organs and intestines are burnt, so that smoke issues from your sense-organs (eyes, nose, mouth, etc). The second one is called Mud Of Putrid Corpses Hell. The ground is a collection of impure substances into which you fall, flip-flop, so that all the dirty, impure substances enter into all of your sense organs (mouth, nose, etc.) and in this way you suffer. Also, in this mud is a large collection of worms with iron lips which bore and cut into all your limbs and every part of your body, right down to the bones. In this way you suffer terribly. The third is called the Path of Blades Hell. This hell itself has many sectors. Having first crossed the Mud of Putrid Corpses Hell, you enter a plain filled with very sharp, pointed knife blades. Walking on these, the flesh and bones of your feet are cut to pieces, and thus you suffer. Next, having crossed the mud as before, you find yourself at the forest of sword-leaves. The branches of all the trees are made of weapons, such as swords. In order to seek refuge from the heat which arises because of the power of your karma, you enter the forest. Then a wind comes to stir the trees, which causes all the weapons to fall onto you. Your whole body is cut into many pieces, and so you suffer greatly. Next, you go to the Mountain of Faces. Thinking of getting to the top of this very high mountain, you start to climb it, but you are cut and pierced as you walk upon eight- and sixteen-inch stakes of iron. Having arrived at the top of the mountain, you are met by ravens and kites with iron beaks which pierce your eyes and mouth and eat out your brains. Again, you think of getting to the bottom of the mountain, and so you descend. You walk on the upward-pointing iron stakes which pierce your body. Then, at the bottom of the mountain, there are iron jackals, dogs, wolves and the like who eat your limbs and tear your body into many pieces so that you suffer. Also, in these neighbouring hells and those of short duration your body and tongue are stretched out on a ground of burning iron and held in place by spikes, and upon this [the guardians of hell] plough them up. The fourth is called the Unfordable River Of Hot Ash. Having crossed the plain of stakes, you enter the river of hot ash, where your body is completely burnt. [You wish to leave this] but it is surrounded by the hell guardians, and so you suffer.

Thinking of the sufferings of these hells and wishing to be free from them, you consider the need to practise the holy Dharma. Contemplate and meditate on this again and again.

ii. The Suffering of the Hungry Ghosts: To consider the suffering of the hungry ghosts, there are the external obscurations, internal obscurations and obscuration of food and drink which is called the obscuration of obscuration. First, the external obscuration. Because of the power of having performed non-virtuous deeds, such as [those compelled by] avarice, you are born into the land of hungry ghosts. Though you are stricken by hunger and thirst, you are not even able to see food and drink. Sometimes, from a great distance, you see a mountain of rice or a great river. Thinking of going there, you set off, but because of the great distance and the difficult path you experience both mental and physical suffering. When you finally arrive there what appeared to be a mountain of rice is now seen to be either a white rock or a heap of white earth. What appeared to be the river is now seen to be either a mirage or blue slate. Since you cannot satisfy your hunger and thirst, you suffer terribly. Secondly, the internal obscurations: you suffer as before, but on top of that, even if you do find a little food or drink, since the opening of your mouth is no bigger than the eye of a needle, it cannot enter it. Trying to force it, you tear your mouth and drip blood. Even it food enters, it cannot enter the throat since the throat is as thin as the hair of a horse's tail. There, even if a little food does fall into the stomach, which is as large as a mountain, you are not able to dispel your hunger or fill your stomach, and so again you suffer [because you are hungrier and thirstier now]. Third, the obscuration of food and drink: when roaming in all directions, looking for food, you are met by the overseers of the hungry ghosts who chase and beat you, and thus you suffer. You may find a little food, but then you fear that it will be taken away by others. That little bit you find still causes suffering because it cannot enter your mouth, as described above. Then, also, if it does reach your stomach, it turns to flames of fire, because of the power of previous karma. It burns and scorches your entire body, such as the intestines and internal organs, and you suffer as flames issue from all your sense-organs. Although you suffer terribly, you still need to experience these violent sufferings again and again, until your karma is exhausted. For the sake of not

being born into such a place, you must contemplate and
meditate on the need to practise the pure Dharma, which
leads all living beings on the path to enlightenment.

iii. The Suffering of Animals: When considering the suffering of animals, there are two types: for those who live in
masses in the ocean, and for those who are scattered about.
First, in the outer oceans, many living beings, such as
crocodiles and the like, suffer from living clustered together
where they press upon each other like fermented grain in a
vat of beer. They have do definite place to live as they are
pushed about in all directions by the ocean's waves and
currents. They suffer the anxiety of not being certain
whether they will meet with friendly creatures or not. They
also suffer from large animals eating small ones, or a group
of small ones, such as seasnails, ganging together to pierce
and eat big ones, such as crocodiles. Also, there are some
creatures which live in between land masses where it is so
dark that they are unable to see their own bodies. Living on
top of one another, they find it cramped and heavy. Their
bodies are squeezed together and so, when they search for
food and drink, it also causes suffering as they cannot find
any. Of the second type, those scattered about, some are
animals which depend on men. These animals have to pull
heavy carts, do ploughing, be milked, are tied with iron
chains, are beaten with sticks and hooks, and thus are used
for many types of work. In the end, too, they are just killed
for their flesh. Others also suffer the fate of being sold, driven out (into the wilderness), or being killed for their pearls,
wool, bones and hides. Some animals, such as undomesti-
cated creatures which do not depend on man, have to roam
about, with no proper home. For their flesh, they are shot
by hunters, and as they are being chased by the hunters'
dogs, they jump off cliffs, and into ravines. Being wounded
in this way, they still seek to escape, but finally they are
caught and killed. Considering the general suffering of animals, which is stupidity, and the individual suffering which

they experience, you must meditate on the necessity to practise the pure Dharma.

b. *The Suffering of Change*

Because of the power of previous deeds, you can be born as a heavenly god, where whatever you wish for arrives, such as good clothes, delicious food, and so on, and where you have limitless pleasures, such as the pleasure of heavenly goddesses. Nevertheless, when the five signs of death and the five signs of death's approach befall gods, their mental suffering is even greater than the suffering of the hells. Then, when you die, you will change from being a master, such as the king of the gods, Indra, to being born as a servant in some household. Having been the child of a god, the sun or moon, where the light of your own abode is able to illumine the four continents, you may have to take birth in the darkness between land masses where you suffer such that you cannot even see your own outstretched hand. Some may change from having been a universal emperor into a servant's servant. Also, within the human race, you can change from being a powerful person into a weak one, or from being a rich person into a poor one. An entire race of people can become extinct. You are fearful whether or not you will meet with hateful enemies, and again you are fearful whether or not you will be separated from pleasing friends. Being unable to obtain what you desire and not being able to fulfil your hopes, you as a human being suffer unimaginably. Even the demi-gods quarrel among themselves and assault each other, cutting their limbs to pieces. These demi-gods who have the nature of hatred have unimaginable mental suffering because of the jealousy they harbour towards the life and prosperity of the gods.

c. *The Suffering of the Conditional Nature of All Things*

There is no end to the activity and work that human beings endeavour to perform, and so many of these are useless or

wasted. You uselessly exhaust your life in making prepara-
tions to undertake various activities, thinking, 'I must do
this activity and that work,' and so on. Then, when the time
of death arrives after having uselessly exhausted yourself in
futile activity, you suffer terribly since you have been
unable to accomplish your wishes. The wealthy experience
the suffering of losing their property to thieves or to those
in power, while the poor suffer from extreme fatigue in trying to obtain sustenance. In brief, birth among any of the six
races of beings within these three realms of existence does
not pass beyond the nature of suffering. Therefore, in order
not to experience any of these kinds of suffering, you must
consider the necessity to practice the pure Dharma, and then
meditate on this.

i. The Law of Cause and Effect: Birth into the world of existence which is endowed with suffering, as has been
explained above, arises from indulgence in non-virtuous
deeds – the cause of suffering. To abandon this [suffering],
you must abandon its cause. In brief, you must meditate on
the idea of relinquishing all non-virtuous deeds, which are
the cause [of the world of existence] and of accomplishing as
many virtuous deeds as possible, however small they may
be. To explain further: you should consider the three
aspects – consideration of non-virtuous deeds, consideration of virtuous deeds, and consideration of neutral deeds.

To Consider Non-virtuous Deeds: When considering non-
virtuous deeds, you should think about the nature of non-
virtuous deeds, the result of non-virtuous deeds, and the
advice on how to abandon them.

The nature of non-virtuous deeds is divided into ten
types. The first is killing. Having produced the thought of
killing, which arises from any of the three poisons (that is,
desire, hatred or ignorance), if you then intentionally kill
any living being – from an insect, like an ant, up to a human
or foetus – then you have performed the act of killing. The

second is stealing. If you take even the husk of a rice grain which is owned by another, then this is stealing. The third is sexual misconduct. If you have sexual relations with a person who is not your marriage partner, with a person who upholds the banner of Dharma, such as a monk or a nun, with one who is holding the eight precepts for that day, with one who is protected by his or her parents, or even with your own husband or wife but at improper times, such as the daytime, then this is considered improper sexual behaviour. These first three are non-virtuous deeds of body. The fourth is lying. Arising from an impure motivation, such as desire, if, for the purpose of deception, you speak to someone who can hear your speech and who can understand it, then you have lied. The fifth is calumny. If, for the purpose of separating two friends, you speak to incite hatred between them, then this is calumnous speech. The sixth is malicious speech. Arising from an impure motivation such as hatred, if you say something very strongly – whether it is true or not – which distresses another's mind, then this is malicious speech. The seventh is idle, irrelevant speech. If you idly gossip much about purposeless events so that it [causes] unsteadiness or becomes an obstacle to the performance of virtue by yourself or others, then this is idle, irrelevant speech. These four are the non-virtuous deeds of speech. The eighth is covetousness. Arising from the motivation of desire, you think that the wealth, power, and so on, of another should be your own. When you desire to obtain another's prosperity for yourself in this manner, then this is [the impure] thought of covetousness. The ninth is ill-will or malicious thought. Arising from the motivation of hatred, if you have an inappropriate thougth, such as may a person be harmed or may he or she experience much suffering, then this is a mind of ill-will or maliciousness. The tenth is wrong views. Arising from the motivation of ignorance, you think that there is no law of karma, no four noble truths, no triple gem, and so on.

Although a teacher describes the holy scriptures, such as 'from the cause of virtuous deeds the result of happiness arises and from non-virtuous deeds suffering arises,' and you do not believe these to be true, then these are wrong views. These last three are non-virtuous deeds of mind.

Next, you should consider the results of these non-virtuous deeds which should be seen from the point of view of this present life and future lives. Corresponding to each of the ten non-virtuous deeds, in this present life [you will meet with such resutls as]: having a short life, being poor, making enemies with your own spouse, being criticized and slandered against, being in discord with your own friends, hearing unpleasant news, not being believed by others who say that whatever you say is unauthoritative and nonsense, not being able to fulfil your wishes, meeting with great fear, and possessing false, wrong views. The result of non-virtuous deeds which will befall you in a future life depends on the amount which you have performed. Therefore, by having indulged in a small number of non-virtuous deeds, you will be born in the animal realm; by having performed a fair number, you will be born in the realm of hungry ghosts; and by having done a large number, you will take birth in the hells.

Finally, you should think about the advice on how to abandon non-virtuous deeds. Since the performance of non-virtue motivated by the three poisons will never go beyond the result of birth into the three lower realms, would it not be appropriate to physically, verbally, and mentally resolve and promise to abandon [all non-virtuous actions] even at the cost of your life?

To Consider Virtuous Deeds: When considering virtuous deeds, you should think about the nature of virtuous actions, the result of virtuous deeds, and the advice on how to accomplish them.

First, having abandoned the ten non-virtuous deeds as explained above, you accomplish the ten virtuous deeds as far as possible based on a motive which is devoid of desire, hatred and ignorance.

Next, corresponding to each of the ten virtuous deeds, temporarily [in this life you will meet with such results as]: having a long life, being very rich, being in accord and harmony with your spouse, obtaining fame in every direction, being on good terms with your friends, having sound organs [of speech, etc.], [others] believing [whatever you say], accomplishing your wishes, being free from fear, and possesssing pure, right views. The final result of the ten virtuous actions [which will befall] you depends on the amount which you have performed. Therefore, by having performed a small, fair or large amount of virtue, you will obtain the results of either a Shravaka, Pratyekabuddha or unsurpassable enlightenment.

Finally, you should think about the advice on how to accomplish virtue. Since you are able to gain any of the three types of enlightenment by the performance of the ten virtuous deeds, whereby even through the obtainment of the stage of a Shravaka, you are liberated from the fears of the lower realms of samsara, then why would you not contemplate accomplishing virtue?

To Consider Neutral Deeds: The nature of neutral deeds is those deeds which are performed indifferently, with neither a virtuous nor a non-virtuous motive, such as eating, doing handicrafts, and the like. The result of such deeds is neutral in the sense that they are not able to bring about either happiness or suffering, but only a tendency to perform the same type of activity, such as handicraft work.

Actions of this sort should be transformed into virtuous actions. By the power of your motivation, you can change [a neutral deed into a virtuous one]. For example, you should think that you are eating food in order to feed the worms in your body, or that you are eating in order to strengthen the body so that you can properly listen to, contemplate, and meditate [on the holy Dharma]. You can also transform your sitting or coming and going into virtue. For example, you should think that at the time of going you are going for the purpose of meeting your Guru or of listening to the holy Dharma. Also, when going somewhere you should think that there are images of Buddhas or bodhisattvas on your right side. Thus, with your best side, the right, always placed towards a shrine, you should think that you are circumambulating an image.

3 If you Have Attachment to Your Own Purpose, You Do Not Have the Enlightenment Thought

This means that, having seen all the world of existence to be endowed with suffering, as explained above, you wish to be free from such a place, and for this reason you perform as many of the inferior and middling virtuous deeds as possible in order to obtain the stage of a Shravaka or Pratyekabuddha. Since this will not accomplish your own purpose, nor will it be able to achieve the vast aims of others, and since it will be an obstacle to obtaining complete Buddhahood, it is not proper to seek to provide for your own purposes alone. Therefore, for the sake of all sentient beings you must obtain the stage of full and perfect enlightenment or Buddhahood. This state will not arise from incomplete and wrong causes and conditions. For example, if you plant a rice seed at an inappropriate time when there is no heat and moisture, such as during the winter, then the seed will not grow. Also, if, wishing for rice, you should plant a barley seed, then a crop of rice would not grow. Desirous of a rice crop, if you plant the cause, the rice seeds, and collect the conditions – water, fertilizer, heat and moisture – then a rice crop will grow. Similarly, to produce complete and perfect enlightenment [the right and complete causes and conditions are needed]. As it says in the *Nam Nang Ngon Chang* [a Carya Tantra text],

> Through the cause which arises from great compassion, the root which arises from the enlightenment thought, and the conditions [which arise from] skilful means, one becomes fully accomplished [i.e. arrives at the stage of Buddhahood].

In order to practise what has just been quoted, you must meditate on loving kindness, meditate on compassion, meditate on the enlightenment thought, and observe the precepts of the bodhisattva's behaviour.

1. *Loving Kindness*

In order to practise loving kindness, you must meditate upon your relatives, those to whom you are indifferent, your enemies, and all sentient beings. (Also, when meditating upon relatives, it is good to meditate on your mother first). So, first you should know or recognize your mother, remember her kindness, and then meditate on loving kindness for her.

First, to know your mother: you should reflect that this woman who is your present mother has not only been your mother in this life, but has acted as your mother in many other previous lifetimes. As Master Nagarjuna said in his *Letter To King Gautamiputra,* 'The earth would not suffice, for making pills the size of juniper seeds, to equal the number of mothers one has had.' Also, in one sutra it says,

> There is not even enough water in the four oceans to equal the amount of milk that one mother has given us; and even the world of Brahma would be overtowered by those who have acted as one's father if they were arranged like horses and elephants placed one upon another.

Thus [you should understand who your mother is] from these quotations.

Second, to remember her kindness: each time this person has been your mother, she has given you limitless benefits. During the nine or ten months you spent in her womb, she bore the discomfort of heaviness and tiredness. She patiently endured the pain of your birth, even at the risk of her own life. Once born, you were like a wriggling worm, neither knowing anything nor having the ability to do anything, but with a loving heart she protected and cared for you. Looking on you with loving eyes, she fed you delicious food with her own tongue, cleaned your dirt with her own hands, cradled you in her ten fingers, gave you as much food and clothing as she possibly could, and protected you from all harm. When you were grown up, she gave you all her precious things, even risking her own life [for your benefit], and taught you all forms of knowledge, such as reading and writing. In brief, she has given you every benefit and protected you from every harm, so you must think about her kind and compassionate acts.

Third, to meditate on loving kindness for your mother: As Master Chandrakirti said, 'Great loving kindness is said to be the way to accomplish benefit for living beings.'

As he said, the nature of loving kindness is the benevolent mind which thinks, 'May all sentient beings have happiness and the cause of happiness.' Therefore, you should first produce loving kindness which is linked with the creation of the enlightenment thought, thus: 'I must ensure that my kind mother has happiness and the cause of happiness.' Then you should produce loving kindness, which is linked with intention, thus, 'I wish that she may have happiness and the cause of happiness.' Finally, you should produce loving kindness, which is linked with prayer, thus, 'May she have happiness and the cause of happiness.' With an unwavering, undistracted mind, meditate in this way and also recite these words.

Just as you recognized your present mother, remembered

her kindness and meditated on loving kindness for her in the above way, now you should transfer these thoughts towards those to whom you are indifferent, to your enemies and to all sentient beings, and meditate upon them.

2. *Compassion*

If you train well by meditating on loving kindness in this way, then through the power of this practice compassion will arise. As it is said [in a sutra], 'The water of compassion [courses through the canal of] loving kindness, and that [compassion] is rightly born from suffering.'

To meditate upon compassion you should understand the nature of compassion, which is explained by Master Chandrakirti, thus, 'Completely saving living beings who are endowed with suffering is said to be great compassion.'

As he said, when you see an object of suffering, there is produced in your mind the desire for that living being to be free from unbearable suffering.

To meditate on compassion you should direct your meditation towards your relatives, those to whom you are indifferent, to your enemies, and to all sentient beings. First, when meditating on your mother, first recognize who she is and remember her kindness just as you did at the time of meditating on loving kindness. Then meditate on compassion for her in the following way. You should visualize your present mother – whether living or dead – clearly in front of you, and think: 'Since my very kind mother possesses suffering and is parted from happiness, I must have compassion for her. Though she desires to be free from suffering and the cause of suffering, I see her present condition to be endowed with suffering and its cause. Since she partakes of more suffering, I must have compassion for her. Therefore, I must make my mother free from this kind of suffering and its cause.' So you should meditate upon compassion, which is linked with the enlightenment thought for her. Then, as at the time of meditating on loving kindness, you should meditate on compassion [linked with intention and prayer].

Then you should transfer this compassion meditation to those to whom you are indifferent, to your enemies and to all sentient beings one after another. In this way, you should continue to meditate until real, unartificial mind of compassion arises.

3. *The Enlightenment Thought*

Through the power of compassion which has been properly produced in this way, the thought of enlightenment will arise. As it is said [in a sutra], 'The root of that [enlightenment thought] is compassion. It is the mind which desires to benefit sentient beings always.'

Thus, as it says, you must embark on the relative enlightenment thought whereby you meditate, exchanging your own self for others. Seeing all sentient beings who are as vast as space as the object of your meditation, recite words such as:

> May the sufferings of all sentient beings ripen upon me, and through my virtues may they all obtain happiness,
> or
> Whatever sufferings and mental sufferings are possessed by all sentient beings who are as vast as space, may all of these ripen upon me. Whatever virtues, happiness, good qualities and articles I have, may all of these be obtained by all sentient beings.

Reciting these words and with a sincere and resolved mind, you should meditate.

4. *Precepts for the Practice of the Bodhisattvas*

Generally, the practice of behaviour of the bodhisattvas is to abandon harming others and to accomplish as much benefit as possible for others. In particular, the bodhisattva must practise the six perfections (of giving, moral conduct, patience, diligence, meditation, and wisdom) in order to mature their own mind, and they must accomplish the four means of gathering adherents (which are giving, speaking pleasantly, encouraging others to practise according to their abilities, and practising properly oneself in order to encourage others to practise) in order to mature others. In the *Akashagarbha Sutra, Sikshasamuccaya, Bodhicaryavatara,* and *Ratnavali* the manner *of* practising the precepts is explained in great detail.

4   *If Grasping Arises, You Do Not Have the View*

This means that although you have produced the relative enlightenment thought well, you have done so at the same time as grasping phenomena as being true. In this way you fall into the extremes of eternalism or nihilism, and so are not able to gain liberation. Therefore, in order to overcome grasping at substantiality and at attributes or characteristics, you must meditate on concentration-meditation and insight wisdom. As it is said,

> Knowing that the faults of the afflictions are destroyed by insight wisdom which is well endowed with concentration-meditation, first one must seek [to obtain] concentration-meditation. This, also, will be perfectly accomplished by non-attachment to the world [or worldly activities].

In order to practise this, you must meditate on concentration-meditation, insight wisdom, and the two together.

1. *Concentration-meditation (Samatha)*

Having found a place which is free from the 'thorns' of

meditation, such as a secluded, pleasant place which is under the protection of a Dharma king and free from the harm and obstacles of the comings and goings of people, you should sit on a comfortable seat. As a preliminary practice for every meditation session, you should take refuge and create the thought of enlightenment. Then place the feet in the vajra posture, the hands in the meditation posture, the tip of the tongue slightly touching the palate, the spine erect and straight, and the eyes half closed: this is the proper position for meditation. As Lord Maitreya said,

> Having settled the body in the right place, concentration-meditation is used to rest the mind upon the mind [so that it remains undistracted] and insight wisdom is used to penetrate into the real nature of all things.

Thus, as he says, you should place your mind one-pointedly on an object of meditation – whether it be a mental object or an external physical object like a black pebble – and this is the practice of concentration-meditation. In the *Samadhiraja Sutra*, the Elder Uttara Bhadra said that one should meditate on an image [or the visualization] of the Buddha. Although there is no difference in the method of placing the mind one-pointedly while concentrating on an image of the Buddha or a black pebble, since, when visualizing an image of the Buddha, you also bring to mind the recollection of the Buddha, more merit is produced. This latter method is therefore used here. In the space in front of you, visualize a jewelled throne upon which is a multi-coloured lotus and a moon disc. Seated upon that is the Buddha Shakyamuni, whose body is yellow in colour, like pure gold. His right hand is in the earth-touching gesture and his left hand is in the meditation posture. Wearing saffron-coloured robes, he sits with His feet in the vajra position. You should meditate with this visualization. You should visualize His whole body, and especially direct your visualization to the tuft of hair in between His eyebrows, and thus meditate. Alternatively, it is permissible to meditate on the visualization of the Buddha Amitabha whose body is red, with His two hands in the meditation posture, with the throne, and so on, being the same as with the visualization of the Buddha Shakyamuni. Therefore, before proceeding to insight wisdom, you must meditate on concentration-meditation, because the meaning of the previous quotation, 'first one must seek [to obtain] concentration-meditation', is this. When you can meditate well on concentration-meditation then you can transfer your meditation to any object. When you are able to rest your mind upon any object for months or even years, this is proper concentration-meditation. However, this [concentration-meditation] alone is not sufficient to remove the afflictions. The antidote for this is insight wisdom. Having examined the true nature of all mental and physical phenomena through discriminating wisdom, the mind, which realizes the state devoid of all extreme views such as existence and non-existence, permanence and nothingness, and so forth [has attained] insight wisdom. The method of placing the mind one-pointedly was previously explained as concentration-meditation, and insight wisdom was then explained later. Now that which is seen through insight wisdom must be placed one-pointedly [before the mind) through concentration-meditation.

2. Insight Wisdom (Vipassana)

The meditation on insight wisdom consists of three parts: establishing all outer appearance as being made by mind, establishing the mind as being illusory, and establishing the illusion as being devoid of an inherent nature of its own.

First, to establish all outer appearances as being made by mind. All the different outer appearances or visions which we see, such as horses, elephants, men, women, vases, cloth, and so on, did not arise without a cause, nor were they made by chance, God, the four elements, atoms, or the manifestation of the Buddha. These appearances arise from the power of placing the propensities or impressions of this or that [object] upon our own mind since beginningless time. [Your own] mind is the creator of all these [appearances]. You must realize that there is no other creator of these than your own mind. You must meditate on this idea.

Second, establishing the mind as being illusory. As it says in the *Samadhiraja Sutra,*

> Just as the appearance of the various illusory
> forms of horses, elephants and carts made by
> magicians are not true in any way, just so should
> all dharmas be known.

Just as it says, all the different outer appearances previously explained are like a dream or magical illusion. For example, although you may experience various joys or sorrows in a dream, everyone knows these do not truly exist. Therefore, you should reflect that these appearances which are just at the relative, apparent level of existence are like the reflection of images seen in a mirror. Until you have a certain knowledge of this [or a faith or a sense that this is so], you must meditate again and again.

Third, to establish the illusion as being devoid of an inherent nature of its own. In this way, although these appearances – the various appearances which are like illusory objects – merely relatively, apparently exist, still their appearance is unceasing. However, should they be examined at the level of ultimate truth, nothing would be found to exist – not even as much as a hundredth part of a hair's tip. You must meditate on this idea.

3. *The Merging of Concentration-meditation and Insight Wisdom*

Having established, step by step, that all appearances are mind-made, that this mind is illusory and that the illusion is without an inherent, true nature of its own, you have arrived, with absolute certainty, at the realization that all things are emptiness, a state totally free from all mentally-created extremes [such as existence, non-existence, both existence and non-existence, or neither existence nor non-existence]. Merging the mind which realizes this and the true nature of objects non-dually together so that they are of one taste, like water poured into water or melted butter mixed into melted butter, you should meditate with the mind placed one-pointedly upon this. By constantly meditating in this way you will become habituated [to the truth], and non-referential compassion which is brought about through [the realization of] emptiness will be produced for those sentient beings who have not realized this. Further, the erroneous view of grasping things to be true disappears and all illusory visions appear as primordial wisdom. Thus, you will manifestly arrive at the stage of complete enlightenment which is endowed with the three bodies (kaya) of perfection.

5 Conclusion and Dedication of Merit

At the conclusion of each meditation session, you should dedicate the root of virtue arising from the meditation on profound samadhi, and also whatever root of virtue you and others have gathered in all the directions through conditional causes. The aim of your dedication is to gain the stage of omniscient Buddhahood. The dedication is directed for the sake of all sentient beings, who are equal to space. The dedication is performed with the understanding that these [merits together with their dedication] are like a dream and a magical illusion. Having first considered these aspects [then recite the dedication thus]:

> By this virtue, may all living beings collect the accumulations of merit and transcendental knowledge, and may they obtain the two holy bodies which arise from merit and transcendental knowledge.

Thus you should recite whatever dedication prayers you know from the sutras and other authoritative scriptures.

Part Seven
Conclusion

Religious Values and Human Society
His Holiness, Tenzin Gyatso, the Fourteenth Dalai Lama

Broadly speaking, there are two types of happiness and suffering, mental and physical, and of the two I believe that mental suffering and happiness are the more acute. Hence I stress the training of the mind to endure suffering and attain a more lasting state of happiness. However, I also have a more general and concrete idea of happiness: a combination of inner peace, economic development, and, above all, world peace. To achieve such goals I feel it is necessary to develop a sense of universal responsibility, *a deep concern for all, irrespective of creed, colour, sex, or nationality.*

The Dalai Lama

Introduction to Part Seven

In this final section we listen to a man who more than anyone else today stands as the living symbol and personification of the Tibetan Buddhist tradition. Here, His Holiness the Dalai Lama addresses some of the most basic issues that humankind faces in this present world. He speaks directly and simply, leaving aside traditional religious terminology, and seeks to awaken in us the fundamental human qualities of compassion, tolerance, justice and honesty.

This talk was given during His Holiness's 1979 tour of the United States, in Constitution Hall, Washington D.C. It was translated by Jeffrey Hopkins (although much of what is said is probably in His Holiness's own English) and was published in 1984 as part of a collection of teachings entitled *Kindness, Clarity and Insight*. For an illuminating presentation of the Dalai Lama's views on the unity of the different Tibetan Buddhist traditions, see the final chapter of this same book, a lecture called *Union of the Old and New Translation Schools*.

Religious Values and Human Society

In one way – in material terms – this present generation has reached a high level of development. Yet, at the same time, we human beings are facing many problems. Some are due to external events or causes, such as natural disasters. These we cannot avoid. However, many problems are created by our own mental defects: we suffer because of an internal lack. I call these problems unnecessary ones, for if we adopt a right mental attitude, these man-made problems need not arise.

Often they are due to differences in ideology, and unfortunately different religious faiths are also sometimes involved. Hence it is very important that we have a right attitude. There are many different philosophies, but what is of basic importance is compassion, love for others, concern for others' suffering, and reduction of selfishness. I feel that compassionate thought is the most precious thing there is. It is something that only we human beings can develop. And if we have a good heart, a warm heart, warm feelings, we will be happy and satisfied ourselves, and our friends will experience a friendly and peaceful atmosphere as well. This can be experienced nation to nation, country to country, continent to continent.

The basic principle is compassion, love for others. Underlying all is the valid feeling of 'I,' and on a conventional level, there is an I – 'I want this,' 'I do not want that.' We experience this feeling naturally, and naturally we want happiness – 'I want happiness,' 'I do not want suffering.' Not only is it natural, it is right. It needs no further justification; it is a natural feeling validated simply by the fact that we naturally and correctly want happiness and do not want suffering.

Based on that feeling, we have the right to obtain happiness and the right to get rid of suffering. Further, just as I myself have this feeling and this right, so others equally have the same feeling and the same right. The difference is that when you say 'I,' you are speaking of just one single person, one soul. Others are limitless. Thus, you should visualize the following: on one side imagine your own 'I' which so far has just concentrated on selfish aims. On the other side imagine others – limitless, infinite beings. You yourself are a third person, in the middle, looking at those on either side. As far as the feeling of wanting happiness and not wanting suffering, the two sides are equal, absolutely the same. Also, with regard to the right to obtain happiness they are exactly the same. However, no matter how important the selfishly motivated person is, he or she is only one single person; no matter how poor the others are, they are limitless, infinite. The unbiased third person naturally can see that the many are more important than the one. Through this, we can experience, can feel, that the majority – the other limitless beings – are more important than the single person 'I.'

Thus, the question is: should everyone be **used for my** attainment of happiness, or should I be used to gain **happiness** for others? If I am used for these infinite beings, it is right. If others are used for this single I, it is **absolutely** wrong. Even if you can use these others, you will **not be** happy, whereas if this one single 'one' contributes, serves as much as he or she can, that is a source of great joy. It is in terms of this attitude that real compassion and love for others can be developed.

Compassion which is based on such reasoning and feelings can be extended even to one's enemies. Our ordinary sense of love and compassion is actually very much involved with attachment. For your own wife or husband, your parents, your children, you have a feeling of compassion and love. But because it is in fact related to attachment, it cannot include your enemies. Again it is centred on a selfish motivation – because these are *my* mother, *my* father, *my* children, I love them. In contrast to this is a clear recognition of the importance and rights of others. If compassion is developed from that viewpoint, it will reach even to our enemies.

In order to develop such a motivation of compassion, we must have tolerance, patience. In the practice of tolerance, one's enemy is the best teacher. Your enemy can teach you tolerance whereas your teacher or parents cannot. Thus, from this viewpoint, an enemy is actually very helpful – the best of friends, the best of teachers.

In my own experience, the period of greatest gain in knowledge and experience is the most difficult period in one's life. If you go along in an easy way, with everything okay, you feel everything is just fine. Then one day, when you encounter problems, you feel depressed and hopeless. Through a difficult period you can learn, you can develop inner strength, determination and courage to face the problem. Who gives you this chance? Your enemy.

This does not mean that you obey or bow down to your enemy. In fact, sometimes, according to the enemy's attitude, you may have to react strongly – but, deep down, calmness and compassion must not be lost. This is possible. Some people may think, 'Now the Dalai Lama is talking nonsense,' but I am not. If you practise this, if you test it by your own experience, you can feel it yourself.

The development of love and compassion is basic, and I usually say that this is a key message of religion. When we speak of religion, we need not refer to deeper philosophical issues. Compassion is the real essence of religion. If you try to implement, to practice, compassion, then as a Buddhist, even if you do not place much emphasis on the Buddha, it is all right. For a Christian, if you try to practice this love, there is no need for much emphasis on other philosophical matters. I say this in a friendly way. The important thing is that in your daily life you practise the essential things, and on that level there is hardly any difference between Buddhism, Christianity, or any other religion. All religions emphasize betterment, improving human beings, a sense of brotherhood and sisterhood, love – these things are common. Thus, if you consider the essence of religion, there is not much difference.

I myself feel and also tell other Buddhists that the question of nirvana will come later. There is not much hurry. But if in day-to-day existence you lead a good life, honestly, with love, with compassion, with less selfishness, then automatically it will lead to nirvana. In contrast, if you talk about nirvana, talk about philosophy, but do not bother much about day-to-day practice, then you may reach a strange nirvana but will not reach the correct nirvana because your daily practice is nothing.

We must implement these good teachings in daily life. Whether you believe in God or not does not matter so much, whether you believe in Buddha or not does not matter so much; as a Buddhist, whether you believe in reincarnation or not does not matter so much. You must lead a good life. And a good life does not mean just good food, good clothes, good shelter. These are not sufficient. A good motivation is what is needed: compassion, without dogmatism, without complicated philosophy; just understanding that others are human brothers and sisters and respecting their rights and human dignity. That we humans can help each other is one of our unique human capacities. We must share in other peoples' suffering; even if we cannot help with money, to show concern, to give moral support and express sympathy are themselves valuable. This is what should be the basis of our lives; whether we call it religion or not does not matter.

In the current world atmosphere, some people may think that religion is for those who remain in remote places and is not much needed in the spheres of business or politics. My answer to this is 'No!' For, as I have just said, in my simple religion, love is the key motivation. Except for certain minor ones, all actions – all larger and deliberate actions – come with motivation. In politics, if you have a good motivation and with that motivation seek to better human society, you are a good and honest politican. Politics itself is not bad. We speak of 'dirty politics,' but this is not right. Politics is necessary as an instrument to solve human problems, the problems of human society. It itself is not bad; it is necessary. However, if politics is practised by bad people, out of cunning and lacking the right motivation, then of course it becomes bad.

This is true not only of politics but in all areas, including religions – if I speak of religion with a bad motivation, that preaching becomes bad. But you cannot say religion is bad; you cannot speak of 'dirty religion.'

Thus, motivation is very important, and thus my simple religion is love, respect for others, honesty: teachings that cover not only religion but also the fields of politics, economics, business, science, law, medicine – everywhere. With proper motivation these can help humanity; without it they go the other way. Without good motivation, science and technology, instead of helping, bring more fear and threaten global destruction. Compassionate thought is very important for humankind.

At the present moment, if you look more deeply into society, you see that people are not as happy as might first seem. For example, when I first land in a new country, everything is very beautiful. When I meet new people, everything is very nice, no complaints at all. But then, day by day I listen, I hear peoples' problems, and it is clear that everywhere there are many problems. Deep down there is unrest. Because of this inner feeling of unrest, people feel isolated, they get depressed, have mental uneasiness, mental suffering. This is the general atmosphere. Real justice and honesty are impossible within cunning feelings. Wanting to benefit others but deep down having a selfish motivation is again impossible. If you talk about peace, love, justice, etc., but then when things are actually affecting you, forget all about them and, if necessary, suppress others or even make war, this is a clear sign that something is lacking.

This troubled atmosphere is our current reality. It is very bad, but it is reality. People may feel that the opposite of this, the internal transformation about which I have been speaking, is merely idealistic and not related to our situation here on earth. My feeling, however, is that if this present atmosphere in which everything depends on money and power and there is not much concern about the real value of love continues, if human society loses the value of justice, the value of compassion, the value of honesty, we will in the next generation or farther in the future face greater difficulties and more suffering. Thus, although to bring about inner change is difficult, it is absolutely worthwhile to try. This is my firm belief. What is important is that we try our best. Whether we succeed or not is a different question. Even if we cannot achieve what we seek within this life, it is all right; at least we will have made the attempt to form a better human society on the basis of love – true love – and less selfishness.

The people who deal daily with current problems must focus on the immediate problem but at the same time must look at the long-term effect on humankind, on human society. For example, basically, your whole physical body must be healthy and strong, for, with a basis of good health, you will not experience minor illness or, even if you do, can within a short period easily be cured. Human society is similar. If we concentrate one hundred percent in the 'realistic way' on short-term benefits, on a temporary-benefits-basis, this is like being sick today and taking a pill. If at the same time there is more thought and more discussion about the long-term future of humankind, this is like building a healthy body. It is necessary to combine temporary and long-term handling of problems.

For the last several years I have been looking at the world's problems, including our own problem, the Tibetan situation. I have been thinking about this and meeting with people from different fields and different countries. Basically all are the same. I come from the East; most of you here are Westerners. If I look at you superficially, we are different, and if I put my emphasis on that level, we grow more distant. If I look on you as my own kind, as human beings like myself, with one nose, two eyes, and so forth, then automatically that distance is gone. We are the same human flesh. I want happiness; you also want happiness. From that mutual recognition we can build respect and real trust for each other. From that can come co-operation and harmony, and from that we can prevent many problems.

In this world at the present moment, not just nation to nation, but continent to continent, we are heavily dependent upon each other. Hence it is essential that there be true co-operation with good motivation. Then we can solve many problems. Good relations, heart to heart, human to human, are very important and very necessary. Everything depends upon good motivation.

Glossary

Glossary

Abiding nature. (Tib. gnas.lugs.) The way in which something actually exists as opposed to the way it appears to exist to a deluded mind.

Abiding tranquillity. (Skt. samatha. Tib. zhi.gnas.) A steady, one-pointed state of concentration. The foundation for insight.

Abhisekha. (Skt., Tib. dhang.) A tantric initiation or empowerment.

Absolute bodhi-mind. A bodhisattva's direct realization of the ultimate truth of emptiness.

Acala. (Skt., Tib. mi.gyo.ba.) 'The Immovable One.' The name of a tantric deity.

Action tantra. (Skt. kriyatantra, Tib. bya.rgyud.) The first of the four classes of tantra.

Affliction. (Skt. klesa, Tib. nyon.mongs.) Any emotion or conception which disturbs and distorts consciousness. The six root afflictions are attachment, anger, self-importance, ignorance, afflicted views and afflicted doubt.

Aggregate. (Skt. skandha, Tib. phung.po.) There are five aggregates: form, feeling, discernment, formative elements and consciousness. This is a basic five-fold categorization of physical and mental phenomena. It is principally used to describe the body-mind complex.

Aggregate faculty. See 'Aggregate.'

Aksobhya. (Skt., Tib. mi.bskyod.pa.) 'The Unshakable One.' One of the five dhyani Buddhas.

Amrita. (Skt., Tib. bdud.rtsi.) Literally, 'deathlessness.' Conventionally understood as the divine ambrosia or nectar of the gods.

Analytical meditation. (Tib. dpyad.sgom.) Repeated conceptual examination of the object which precedes one-pointed concentration meditation.

Anti-god. (Skt.asura., Tib. hla.ma.yin.) A class of celestials afflicted with jealousy who are in a constant state of conflict with the higher celestials. One of the six realms within samsara.

Apsara. (Skt.) A local spirit.

Arhat. (Skt., Tib. dgra.bcom.pa.) A liberated saint who is free from the afflictions and has attained nirvana.

Arya. (Skt. tib. 'phags.pa.) Literally, 'A Noble One.' One who has progressed along the spiritual path to the point where he or she has a direct realization of ultimate truth.

Avalokiteshvara. (Skt., Tib. spyan.ras.gzigs.) A bodhisattva who personifies the compassion of enlightenment.

Avici Hell. The hell of uninterrupted torment. The lowest of the eight hot hells.

Bardo. (Tib., Skt. anubhava.) The intermediate state between death and rebirth.

Birthlessness. Ultimate truth, the unconditioned, nirvana.

Bodhicitta. (Skt., Tib. byang.chub.kyi.sems.) The altruistic resolve to attain enlightenment for the sake of all sentient beings. The foundation of Mahayana Buddhism.

Bodhi-mind. See 'Bodhicitta.'

Bodhisattva. (Skt., Tib. byang.chub.sems.dpa'.) A being who has cultivated bodhicitta and has dedicated his or her life to the attainment of enlightenment for the benefit of all sentient beings.

Body of essential nature. (Skt. svabhavikakaya, Tib. ngo.bo. nyid.sku.) The ultimate reality of a Buddha's mind.

Body of pristine awareness. (Skt. jnanadharmakaya, Tib. ye.shes. chos.sku.) The mind of a Buddha, the spiritual core of Buddhahood.

Body that subsumes everything. (Skt. dharmakaya, Tib. chos.sku.) A general term which covers both the body of essential nature and the body of pristine awareness. Sometimes used to refer exclusively to a Buddha's state of being; sometimes it refers to the ultimate nature of reality itself.

Buddha-nature. (Skt. tathagatagarbha, Tib. sangs.rgyas.kyi.rigs.) The potential every sentient being has to realize Buddhahood. The Buddha essence within each being which is uncovered through enlightenment.

Celestial. (Skt. deva, Tib. hla.) The highest of the six classes of beings within samsara.

Chakra. (Skt., Tib. 'khor.lo.) Literally, 'wheel.' One of five principal points in the subtle body where the energy channels meet and are interconnected.

Chakrasamvara. (Skt., Tib. 'khor.lo.bde.mchog.) The name of a deity belonging to the class of the supreme yoga tantra. A tantric form of Avalokiteshvara.

Chandali. (Skt., Tib. gtum.mo.) The 'inner warmth' generated through tantric practice as part of the completion stage.

Chittamatra. (Skt., Tib. sems.tsam.) Literally, 'Mind Only.' The name of a Mahayana Buddhist school of philosophy which maintains that the whole of reality is nothing but the nature of mind.

Chöd. (Tib.) Literally 'cutting.' A powerful tantric practice aimed at severing attachment to the ego.

Clear light. (Skt. abhasvara, Tib. 'od.gsal.) The fundamental and ultimate nature of mind.

Closed-mindedness. (Skt. moha, Tib. gti.mug.) One of the three mental poisons (the other two being attachment and anger). The delusion, dullness and stupidity which confuse the mind.

Cognitive base. (Skt. ayatana, Tib. skyes.mched.) The six senses (sight, hearing, etc.) and the six objects of the senses (forms, sounds, etc.) which act as the bases for consciousness.

Community. (Skt. sangha, Tib. dge.'dun.) The third of the three jewels of refuge. In its deepest sense the spiritual community includes only those who have reached the stage of an arya. Generally, it is used to refer to the community of monks and nuns or, in the Mahayana, of bodhisattvas.

Complacent liberation. The state of liberation from samsara in which one remains quiescently absorbed in the bliss of nirvana. The liberation of an arhat as opposed to a Buddha.

Completion stage. (Skt. utpattikrama, Tib. rdzogs.rim.) The second and final stage of practice according to the supreme yoga tantra.

Concentration-meditation. (Tib. 'jog.sgom.) The stage which succeeds analytical meditation where one focuses the mind one-pointedly on the object of reflection.

Contemplation. (Skt. cinta, Tib. bsam.pa.) The reflection upon what has been learnt which precedes one-pointed meditation.

Conventional mind. (Tib. kun.rdzob.pa'i.sems.) The mind which is conscious of conventional truths as opposed to the ultimate truth of emptiness.

Creative energy. (Skt. bindu, Tib. thig.le.) Concentrated points c 'drops' of energy present at the subtle level of the body.

Cyclic existence. (Skt. samsara, Tib. Zkhor.ba.) The beginning. cycle of birth and death through which sentient beings are propelled by the force of their actions and afflictions.

Dakini. (Skt., Tib. mkha'.'gro.ma) A class of female divinities propitiated and identified with in tantric practice. The female principle of enlightenment.

Deeds. (Skt. carya, Tib. spyod.pa.) Conduct, behaviour, way of life, as opposed to philosophical or doctrinal attitude.

Deity. See 'Celestial.' The term 'deity' is mainly used to refer to Buddhas and bodhisattvas alone who are visualized in a divine form during tantric practice.

Delusion. See 'Affliction.'

Demi-god. See 'Anti-god.'

Demonic force. (Skt. mara, Tib. bdud.) There are four demonic forces which hinder spiritual development: (1) the aggregates; (2) the afflictions; (3) death; and (4) the celestial Devaputra.

Development stage. (Skt. sampannakrama, Tib. bskyed.rim.) The first of the two stages of supreme yoga tantra.

Devil. See 'Demonic Force.'

Dharma. (Skt., Tib. chos.) The Truth, the way things are. The teachings of the Buddha which reveal this truth. When uncapitalized, phenomena, events.

Dharma body. See 'body that subsumes everything.'

Dharmakaya. See 'body that subsumes everything.'

Dhyani Buddha. A term coined by Western scholars to refer to the five Buddha 'families' (Tib. rgyal.ba.rigs.lnga.). These are the five principal aspects of Buddhahood represented in personified Buddha forms. They correspond to the purified aspects of the five aggregates.

Diamond vehicle. (Skt. vajrayana, Tib. rdo.rje.theg.pa.) The Buddhist path of tantric practice.

Drop of energy. See 'Creative energy.'

Dzog-chen. (Tib., Skt. Maha-ati.) Literally, the 'great perfection' or 'great completion.' One of the highest forms of meditation practice which aims at a direct realization of the ultimate nature of reality.

Effort of armour. (Tib. go.cha'i.brtson.'grus.) A kind of perseverance, the strength of which protects one from hindrances as though it were a spiritual armour.

Ego-grasping. (Tib. bdag.'dzin.) The deeply engrained notion of 'I' which conceives of ego as permanent, independent and partless.

Ego reflection. (Skt. prapanca, Tib. spros.ba.) The habitual proliferation of concepts and mental constructs which tend to dominate mental activity.

Eight faults. The sufferings of birth, sickness, ageing, death, being separated from what is dear to us, encountering what is not dear to us, not obtaining what we want, and the difficulty of keeping our possessions.

Eight liberties. Being free from the following eight conditions: (1) birth as a hell-being; (2) birth as a hungry ghost; (3) birth as an animal; (4) birth as a barbarian; (5) birth as a long-lived celestial; (6) birth as one with erroneous views; (7) birth at a time when no Buddha has appeared; and (8) birth as one devoid of the faculties needed to understand the Dharma.

Eight worldly concerns. (Tib. 'jig.rten.chos.brgyad.) These are gain and loss, fame and disgrace, praise and blame, pleasure and pain.

Eight worldly feelings. See 'Eight worldly concerns.'

Emanation body. (Skt. nirmanakaya, Tib. sprul.sku.) The physical manifestations of a Buddha's presence in the world.

Empowerment. See 'Abhiseka.'

Emptiness. (Skt. shunyata, Tib. stong.pa.nyid.) The mere absence of inherent nature. The ultimate nature of all phenomena.

Energy. (Skt. prana, Tib. rlung.) The subtle 'airs' that course through the body and, according to the tantras, serve as the basis for mental activity.

Energy channel. (Skt. nadi, Tib. rtsa.) The subtle pathways along which the subtle bodily energies run.

Energy current. See 'Energy.'

Energy-wind. See 'Energy.'

Enjoyment body. (Skt. sambhogakaya, Tib. longs.sku.) The subtle manifestations of a Buddha's presence which are only perceived by arya bodhisattvas.

Enlightened motive. See 'Bodhicitta.'

Enlightened thought. See 'Bodhicitta.'

Eternalism. (Skt. sasvatavada, Tib. rtag.lta.) The erroneous view that the self is an unchanging, indestructible entity. An extreme view; the opposite of nihilism.

Examination meditation. See 'Analytical meditation.'

Fearful and angered repulsion. (Skt. dvesa, Tib. che.sdang.) An afflicted mental factor which unrealistically conceives of its object as hateful and bears strong aversion towards it.

Fettering passion. See 'Affliction.'

Five certainties. The five principal characteristics of the enjoyment body. These are: (1) certainty of place (the pure realm called Akanistha); (2) certainty of time (until the end of samsara); (3) certainty of teaching (only the Mahayana); (4) certainty of entourage (only Arya bodhisattvas); and (5) certainty of form (endowed with the major and minor marks of perfection).

Five consorts. (tib. yum.lnga.) The five female counterparts of the five Dhyani Buddhas. They are often symbolically depicted embracing the male Buddha figure.

Five Heinous Crimes. (Tib. mtshams.med.lnga.) These are: (1) killing one's father; (2) killing one's mother; (3) killing an arhat; (4) shedding the blood of a Buddha; and (5) causing a schism in the sangha.

Five poisons. These are attachment, hatred, ignorance, pride and jealousy.

Form body. (Skt. rupakaya, Tib. gzugs.sku.) A general name for the physical manifestations of a Buddha. It is composed of the emanation body and the enjoyment body.

Foundation of everything. (Skt. alaya, Tib. kun.gzhi.) The fundamental ground of reality from which all appearances within samsara and nirvana spring.

Foundation expanse. See 'Foundation of everything.'

Foundation sphere. See 'Foundation of everything.'

Founding stratum. See 'Foundation of everything.'

Four immeasurables. (Tib. tshad.med.bzhi.) These are immeasurable love, compassion, joy and equanimity

Four opponent powers. (Tib. gnyen.po.stobs.bzhi.) These are the power of the objects of refuge, the power of performing wholesome actions, the power of cleansing unwholesome actions, and the power of turning away from whatever actions are unwholesome in the future.

Four types of logic. (Tib. rigs.pa.bzhi.) These are: (1) reasoning which leads one to action; (2) reasoning of contingency (e.g. one must act because any result depends upon its own cause); (3) reasoning which establishes the validity (e.g. of the previous reasoning); and (4) natural reasoning (e.g. heat rises because that is the nature of fire).

Garuda. (Skt., Tib. bya.khyung.) A large mythical bird often depicted holding a snake in its beak.

Geshe. (Tib.) A title given to a monk who has completed extensive studies in Buddhist doctrine and philosophy.

God. See 'Celestial.'

Graded course to enlightenment. (Tib. lam.rim.) Oral and written teachings which describe the different stages along the path to enlightenment and the methods whereby to realize them.

Great completion. See 'Dzog-chen.'

Great Seal. (Skt. mahamudra, Tib. phyag.rgya.chen.po.) A meditation practice aimed at the direct realization of emptiness.

Guhyasamaja. (Skt., Tib. gsang.ba.'dus.pa.) A deity belonging to the class of the supreme yoga tantra.

Guru. (Skt., Tib. bla.ma.) A qualified spiritual teacher.

Guru Rinpoche. 'The Precious Guru.' A title given to Padmasambhava, the Indian tantric master, who helped introduce Buddhism to Tibet in the eighth century.

Hearing. (Skt. sruta, Tib. thos.pa.) The listening to or reading of teachings which precedes their actual contemplation and meditation.

Hevajra. (Skt., Tib. kye.rdo.rje.) A deity belonging to the class of the supreme yoga tantra.

Hinayana. (Skt., Tib. theg.pa.dman.pa.) 'The Lesser Vehicle.' A name given by the Mahayanists to the earlier schools of Buddhism which place emphasis on one's personal attainment of nirvana alone.

Hui Neng. The sixth patriarch of the Chinese Ch'an (Zen) school who lived from 638 to 713.

Hungry ghost. (Skt. preta, Tib. Yi-dvags.) One of the six realms of samsara where beings live tormented by unsatisfied desires.

Identitylessness. (Skt. anatman, Tib. bdag.med.) The absence of an inherently existent self or essence. See 'Emptiness.'

Illusive vision. (Tib.'khrul.snang.) The way in which things mistakenly appear to a mind deluded by ignorance.

In-between-period. See 'Bardo.'

Individual liberation. (Skt. pratimoksa, Tib, so.so.thar.pa.) The sets of vows adopted by Buddhist practitioners – from the vows of a monk to those of a lay-person – as a means to help them proceed along the path to enlightenment.

Inherent awareness. (Skt. svasamvedana, Tib. rang.rig.) The ability of consciousness to be aware of itself.

Inherent nature. (Skt. svabhava, Tib. rang.bzhin.) The deeply-rooted illusion of an unchanging, self-existent essence abiding at the heart of all things.

Initial, intermediate and advanced levels of motivation. (Skt. tripurusha, Tib. skyes.bu.gsum.) The initial level of motivation is that of a person who is concerned merely with a higher rebirth within samsara; the intermediate level of motivation is that of one who is concerned with attaining complete liberation from samsara in nirvana; the advanced level of motivation is that of a bodhisattva who aspires to attain Buddhahood for the sake of all sentient beings.

Initiation. See 'Abhisekha.'

Insight. (Skt. vipassana, Tib. hlag.mthong.) Direct awareness and understanding of the nature of reality.

Insight wisdom. See 'Insight.'

Intensive insight. See 'Insight.'

Intentionality. (Skt. abhipraya, Tib. dgongs.pa.) The inner aim or purpose of the Buddha's activity.

Interdependent origination. (Skt. pratityasamutpada, Tib. rten.-ching.'brel. bar.'byung.ba.) The fundamental law of conditionality or relativity.

Intermediate period. See 'Bardo.'

Jetsun. (Tib.) 'Venerable One.' An honorific epithet given to spiritual teachers.

Kaliyuga. (Skt.) According to Buddhist cosmology, the present age of of decline and degeneration in which we live.

Klesa. See 'Affliction.'

Lama. See 'Guru.'

Lodan Sherab. A Tibetan translator who was responsible for translating many Sanskrit texts into Tibetan. He lived from 1059 to 1109.

Longing desire. (Skt. raga, Tib. 'dod.chags.) An afflicted mental factor which erroneously exaggerates the attractiveness of an object and craves to possess it.

Lotsawa. (Tib.) A translator, specifically one of the original Indian or Tibetan scholars who translated the Buddhist scriptures from Sanskrit into Tibetan.

Luminosity. See 'Clear light.'

Madhyamika. (Skt., Tib. dbu.ma.pa.) A Mahayana Buddhist philosopher who asserts that all phenomena are empty of any inherent nature whatsoever. A school of Mahayana Buddhist philosophy founded on the teachings of Nagarjuna.

Madhyamika Prasangika. (Skt., Tib. dbu.ma.thal.'gyur.pa.) One of the two sub-sects of the Madhyamika school of philosophy (the other being that of the Svatantrika). The Prasangika view is often considered to be the highest Buddhist philosophical position.

Mahakala. (Skt., Tib. nag.po.chen.po.) 'The Great Black One,' a deity belonging to the class of the supreme yoga tantra.

Mahamudra. See 'Great Seal.'

Mahayana. (Skt., Tib. theg.pa.chen.po.) 'The Great Vehicle' of Buddhist practice which emphasizes the attainment of enlightenment for the sake of all others.

Major and minor marks of perfection. The thirty-two major and eighty minor physical characteristics which adorn the body of a Buddha.

Mandala. (Skt., Tib. dkyil.'khor.) The abode or world of a deity. Symbolically depicted as a circular, symmetrical diagram.

Manjushri. (Skt., Tib. 'jam.dpal.dbyangs.) A bodhisattva who personifies the wisdom of enlightenment.

Mantra. (Skt., Tib. sngags.) A group of syllables which express in a condensed, symbolic way the essential qualities of a deity. The speech of a deity.

Mantrayana. (Skt., Tib. gsangs.sngags.kyi.theg.pa.) The Buddhist path of tantric practice. The Vajrayana.

Mara. See 'Demonic force.'

Master practitioner. (Skt. mahasiddha, Tib. grub.thob.chen.po.) An adept who has attained proficiency in tantric practice.

Mental fabrication. See 'Ego reflection.'

Mental quiescence. See 'Abiding tranquillity.'

Merit. (Skt. punya, Tib. bsod.nams.) The positive karmic impressions accumulated through wholesome actions.

Method. (Skt. upaya, Tib. thabs.) The 'extensive' aspect of Buddhist practice comprising compassion, generosity, ethics, etc., as opposed to the 'profound' aspect of wisdom.

Mind of enlightenment. See 'bodhicitta.'

Mindfulness. (Skt. smrti, Tib. dran.pa.) The paying of close attention to an object of contemplation or meditation.

Nagarjuna. The Indian founder of the Madhyamika school of Buddhist philosophy who lived in the second century A.D.

Neutral deeds. Actions which are neither wholesome nor unwholesome and leave neither a positive nor a negative karmic effect.

Nihilism. (Skt. ucchedavada, Tib. chad.lta.) The erroneous view which holds that there is no continuity of consciousness after death, that denies the law of moral causation (karma), and asserts that ultimately nothing exists at all.

Nirmanakaya. See 'Emanation body.'

Omniscience. (Skt. sarvajnana, Tib. thams.cad.mkhyen.pa.) The quality of a Buddha's mind which has complete knowledge of all aspects of reality.

Over-estimation. (Skt. samaropa, Tib. sgro.dgogs.) The quality of mind which imagines something to exist when in fact it does not. Exaggeration; projection.

Own purpose. (Tib. rang.don.) That which is meaningful and desirable for oneself alone. The opposite of 'Purpose of others.'

Passions. See 'Afflictions.'

Path of accumulation. (Skt. sambharamarga, Tib. tshogs.lam.) The first of the five paths to enlightenment during which the practitioner firmly establishes him or herself in the direction of the goal.

Path of accumulation. (Skt. sambharamarga, Tib. tshogs.lam.) The first of the five paths to enlightenment during which the practitioner firmly establishes him or herself in the direction of the goal.

Path of preparation. (Skt. prayogamarga, Tib. sbyor.lam.) The second of the five paths to enlightenment during which the practitioner gains a valid conceptual understanding of reality.

Path of seeing. (Skt. darsanamarga, Tib. mthong.lam.) The third of the five paths to enlightenment during which the practitioner first gains a direct, non-conceptual understanding of reality.

Penetrative insight. See 'Insight.'

Perfections. (Skt. paramita, Tib. pha.rol.tu.phyin.pa.) Literally, 'that which has gone beyond.' There are six perfections which need to be cultivated in Mahayana Buddhism: giving, ethics, patience, effort, concentration, and wisdom.

Performance tantra. (Skt. caryatantra, Tib. spyod.rgyud.) The second of the four classes of tantra.

PHAT (Skt.) An emphatic exclamation often signifying expulsion It is found at the end of certain mantras and is sometimes used alone.

Phenomenology. (Skt. abhidharma, Tib. chos.mngon.pa.) The study of the different constituent elements of reality, the nature of the world, the path to enlightenment, etc. One of the three principal divisions of the Buddhist canon (the other two being the Discourses of the Buddha and Monastic Discipline.

Phenomenon. (Skt. dharma, Tib. chos.) A constituent element of reality. Anything that exists either conventionally or ultimately.

Powerful attainment. (Skt. siddhi, Tib. grub.pa) The common and extraordinary effects derived through tantric practice. The 'common' effects are such things as super-normal powers also realized by non-Buddhists; the 'extraordinary' effects are the attainments of enlightenment and Buddhahood.

Prajña. (Skt., Tib. shes.rab) Wisdom. This ranges from the ability to discriminate correctly betweeen what is true and false to the direct, intuitive insight into reality gained through meditation.

Prana. See 'Energy.'

Precept. (Tib. gdams.ngag.) An oral teaching or advice given by a spiritual teacher.

Primordial Buddha. (Tib. gdod.ma'i.sangs.rgyas.) See 'Buddha-nature.'

Primordial wisdom. (Skt. jñana, Tib. ye.shes.) The fundamental awareness of reality possessed by all sentient beings but temporarily obscured by the afflictions.

Pristine awareness. See 'Primordial wisdom.'

Propensity. (Skt. vasana, Tib. bag.chags.) The positive, negative and neutral tendencies planted in the mind through the force of actions. They are compared to seeds which in the future will ripen in the form of happiness or suffering.

Purpose of others. (Tib. gzhan.don.) That which is meaningful or desirable for others. It is the bodhisattva's intention to realize enlightenment in order to accomplish the 'purpose of others.' The opposite of 'own purpose.'

Raksa. (Skt.) A form of wrathful spirit found in Indian mythology.

Relative bodhi-mind. See 'bodhicitta.'

Relative enlightenment thought. See 'bodhicitta.'

Relative level of existence. (Skt. samvrtisatya, Tib. kun.rdzob. bden.pa.) This covers all existent phenomena other than the ultimate truth of emptiness. Anything that is true for a mind conscious of the multiplicity of phenomena as opposed to emptiness. Relative truth; conventional truth.

Relative level of truth. See 'Relative level of existence.'

Relative reality. See 'Relative level of existence.'

Relative truth. See 'Relative level of existence.'

Renunciation. (Tib. nges.'byung.) The firm resolve to liberate oneself from samsara.

Rinpoche. (Tib.) 'Precious One.' An honorific title given to Tibetan Lamas of high standing, particularly tulkus.

Rupakaya. See 'Emanation body.'

Sacred word of honour. (Skt. samaya, Tib. dam.tshig.) The commitment taken by one who has received a tantric initiation.

Samadhi. (Skt., Tib. ting.nge.'dzin.) One-pointed concentration on a single object in meditation.

Samantabhadra. (Skt., Tib. kun.tu.bzang.po.) 'The Always Good.' The name of a bodhisattva. Sometimes used to refer to the Primordial Buddha.

Samatha. See 'Abiding tranquillity.'

Sambhogakaya. See 'Enjoyment body.'

Samaya. See 'Sacred word of honour.'

Sampannakrama. See 'Development stage.'

Samsara. See 'Cyclic existence.'

Sangha. See 'Community.'

Shantideva. An eighth-century Indian master who composed a seminal text on the practice of Mahayana Buddhism: the *Bodhicaryavatara*.

Sarvastavada. (Skt., Tib. thams.cad.yod.pa.smra.ba.) One of the eighteen original Hinayana schools of Buddhism.

Sautrantika. (Skt., Tib. mdo.sde.pa.) The name of a later Hinayana school of Buddhist philosophy which was concerned with the clarification of logical and epistemological issues.

Secret mantra. (Skt. guhyamantra, Tib. gsangs.sngags.) See 'Mantrayana.'

Self nature. See 'Inherent nature.'

Self preoccupation. (Skt. ahamkara, Tib. nga.rgyal.) Pride. Self-importance.

Siddhi. See 'Powerful attainment.'

Six dharmas of Naropa. (Tib. na.ro.chos.drug.) Six practices belonging to the completion stage of tantra formulated by the Indian master Naropa (1016–1100). They are: (1) mystic heat yoga; (2) illusory body yoga; (3) dream body yoga; (4) clear light yoga; (5) consciousness transference yoga; and (6) bardo yoga.

Sphere. (Skt. dhatu, Tib. khams.) One of the basic eighteen elements of reality described in Buddhist phenomenology. These elements are the six sense organs, the six sense objects, and the six sense consciousnesses.

Spiritual friend. (Skt. kalyanamitra, Tib. dge.ba'i.bshes.gnyen.) One who helps guide the practitioner along the spiritual path. A guru or lama.

Shravaka. (Skt., Tib. nyan.thos.) 'A Hearer.' A follower of the Hinayana path who devoted his life to the attainment of enlightenment by following the instructions of the Buddha.

Shunyata. See 'Emptiness.'

Stage of completion. See 'Completion stage.'

Stage of generation. See 'Development stage.'

Store of meritorious experience. (Tib. bsod.nams.kyi.tshogs.) The merits accumulated through wholesome actions which serve as the sound basis for spiritual development. The cause for the Rupakaya.

Store of sound knowledge. (Tib. ye.shes.kyi.tshogs.) The wisdom accumulated through the practice of insight which serves as the sound basis for spiritual development. The cause for the Dharmakaya.

Suchness. (Skt. tathata, Tib. de.bzhin.nyid.) The true nature of
reality. See 'Emptiness.'

Suffering of change. (Tib. 'gyur.ba'i.sdug.bsngal.) The unsatisfactory nature of everything that is impermanent, even if it
appears for the time being as pleasurable.

Suffering of the conditional nature. (Tib. khyab.pa.'du.byas.
kyi.sdug.bsngal.) The pervasive quality of unsatisfactoriness
which characterizes every aspect of conditioned existence.

Suffering of extensiveness. See 'Suffering of the conditional nature.'

Suffering of suffering. (Tib. sdug.bsngal. gyi.sdug.bsngal.) The
actual sensations of pain, misery, discontent, etc.

Supernatural perception. (Skt. abhijña, Tib. mngon.shes.) The
power attained through meditation to perceive such things as
the thoughts of others, past lives and so forth.

Supreme intention. (Tib. hlag.bsam.) The resolve to take on the
burden of liberating all beings from their suffering oneself.

Supreme yoga tantra. (Skt. Anuttarayogatantra, Tib.rnal.'byor.
bla.na.med.pa'i.rgyud.) The highest of the four classes of
tantra.

Sutra. (Skt., Tib. mdo.) A discourse taught by the Buddha.

Sutrayana. (Skt., Tib. mdo'i.theg.pa.) The path of Buddhist practice based on the teachings contained within the sutras, as
opposed to the tantras.

Tantra. (Skt., Tib. rgyud.) Discourses attributed to the Buddha,
or his manifestations, in which the 'esoteric' practices of the
Vajrayana are explained.

Tara. (Skt., Tib. sgrol.ma.) A female bodhisattva represented in
a number of forms who personifies the feminine aspect of
Buddhahood.

Ten endowments. (Tib. 'byor.ba.bcu.) The ten favourable conditions for the practice of Buddhism. They are: (1) being born as
a human being; (2) being born in a civilized land; (3) having
complete sense faculties; (4) not having committed one of the
five heinous crimes; (5) having faith in the Buddha's teaching;
(6) being in a world where the Buddha has appeared; (7) at a
time when he has taught the Dharma; (8) at a time when his
teaching is still extant; (9) at a time when people are still practising it and; (10) at a time when people have compassion for one
another.

Theravada. (Skt.) One of the eighteen earliest sub-schools of Buddhism. The form of Buddhism practised today in Sri Lanka and South-East Asia. Considered by the Mahayana to represent Hinayana Buddhism.

Thirty-seven facets of the path to perfection. (Skt. bodhipaksikadharma, Tib. byang.chub.kyi.phyogs.kyi.chos.) These are the four foundations of mindfulness, the four right efforts, the four bases of miraculous power, the five spiritual faculties, the five spiritual powers, the seven factors of enlightenment, and the eightfold noble path.

Three aspects. (:Skt. trimandala, Tib. 'khor.gsum.) The three constituents necessary for any action: the doer, the recipient of the act, and the act itself.

Three faults. The suffering of suffering, the suffering of change, and the suffering of the conditional nature.

Three jewels. (Skt. triratna, Tib. dkon.mchog.gsum.) The Buddha, the Dharma and the sangha. The three principles around which a Buddhist focuses and structures his or her life.

Three spheres. See 'Three aspects.'

Torma. (Tib.) A ceremonial cake made of roasted barley flour, butter and other ingredients. It is used as an offering.

Transcendence. See 'Perfections.'

Transcendental knowledge. (Skt. prajnaparamita, Tib. shes.rab. kyi.pha.rol.tu.phyin.pa.) The perfection of wisdom.

Tripitaka. (Skt., Tib. sde.snod.gsum.) The three principal divisions of the Buddhist canon: discourses (sutra), discipline (vinaya) and phenomenology (abhidharma).

Tsampa. (Tib.) Roasted barley flour. The staple food of Tibetans.

Tulku. (Tib., Skt. nirmanakaya) A lama of high attainment who has consciously taken rebirth and has been officially recognized as the reincarnation of his or her predecessor.

Two accumulations. The store of meritorious experience and the store of sound knowledge.

Two stages of tantra practice. The completion stage and the development stage.

Ultimate level of truth. (Skt. paramarthasatya, Tib. don.dam.-bden.pa.) The truth which appears to a mind free of affliction. Emptiness.

Ultimate truth. See 'Ultimate level of truth.'

Under-estimation. (Skt. apavada, Tib. skur.'debs.) The quality of mind which imagines something not to exist when in fact it does.

Upasaka. (Skt., Tib. dge.bsnyen.) A Buddhist lay practitioner.

Upaya. See 'Method.'

Utility body. See 'Enjoyment body.'

Utpattikrama. See 'Completion stage.'

Vaibasika (Skt., Tib. bye.brag.smra.ba) A Hinayana school of Buddhist philosophy.

Vajra. (Skt., Tib. rdo.rje.) Diamond. That which is indestructible. A five- or nine-pronged sceptre used in tantric practice as a symbol of method.

Vajra body. (Skt. vajrakaya, Tib. rdo.rje.sku.) The indestructible spiritual and physical presence of Buddhahood.

Vajradhara. (Skt., Tib. rdo.rje.'chang.) The tantric aspect of Buddha Shakyamuni.

Vajrapani. (Skt., Tib. phyag.na.rdo.rje.) A bodhisattva who personifies the spiritual power of enlightenment.

Vajra posture. (Skt. vajrasana, Tib. rdo.rje.dkyil.dkrungs.) The meditation posture in which both legs are fully crossed.

Vajrasattva. (Skt., Tib. rdo.rje.sems.dpa'.) A bodhisattva who personifies the purity of enlightenment.

Vajrayana. See 'Diamond vehicle.'

Vajrayogini. (Skt., Tib. rdo.rje.rnal.'byor.ma.) A female tantric deity belonging to the class of the supreme yoga tantra. The consort of Chakrasamvara.

Victorious One. (Skt., jina, Tib. rhyal.ba.) A Buddha. One who has gained complete victory over the forces of Mara.

Voidness. see 'Emptiness.'

Warmth. (Skt. usmagata, Tib. drod.) The second of the four sub-stages of the path of preparation.

Waves of inspiration. (Skt. adhisthana, Tib. byin.brlabs.) Blessing; grace. The influence which emanates from an enlightened being and inspires the practitioner in his or her spiritual practice.

Wisdom. See 'Prajña.'

World of existence. See 'Cyclic existence.'

Worm. (Tib. rbu.) A micro-organism.

Yama. (Skt., Tib. gshin.rje.) The Lord of Death. A wrathful figure who personifies death in Indian mythology.

Yamantaka. (Skt., Tib. gshin.rje.gshed.) Literally, 'the enemy of Yama'. A deity belonging to the class of the supreme yoga tantra. The wrathful form of Manjushri.

Yidam. (Tib.) The deity with whom one establishes a personal relationship in tantric practice.

Yoga tantra. (Skt., Tib. rnal.'byor.rgyud.) The third of the four classes of tantras.

Yogin (m), yogini (f). (Skt., Tib. rnal.'byor.pa.) A person engaged in the practice of Buddhism. Specifically, one who has realized the union of abiding tranquillity and insight.

Yuganaddha. (Skt., Yib. zung.'jug.) Literally, 'union.' The state of Buddhahood itself.

Suggestions for Further Reading

Avedon, John, F. *In Exile from the Land of Snows*. London: Wisdom, 1985.

Batchelor, Stephen. *Alone With Others*. New York: Grove, 1983.

Chang, Garma C.C. *The Hundred Thousand Songs of Milarepa*. Boulder: Shambhala, 1977.

Chattopadhyaya, A. *Atisa And Tibet*. Calcutta: R. D. Press, 1967.

Dalai Lama, the Fourteenth. *My Land and my People*. New York: McGraw-Hill, 1962.

——————, *Kindness, Clarity and Insight*. Ithaca: Snow Lion, 1984.

Dargyey, Geshe Ngawang. *Tibetan Tradition of Mental Development*. Dharamsala: LTWA, 1974.

Dowman, Keith. *The Divine Madman*. London: RKP, 1980.

——————, *Sky Dancer*. London: RKP, 1984.

Freemantle, Francesca and Trungpa, Chögyam. *The Tibetan Book of the Dead*. Berkeley: Shambhala, 1975.

sGam.po.pa. Tr. Guenther, H. V. *Jewel Ornament of Liberation*. London: Rider, 1959.

Govinda, Lama Anagarika. *The Way of the White Clouds*. London: Rider, 1966.

——————, *Foundations of Tibetan Mysticism*. London: Rider, 1970.

Guenther, H. V. and Trungpa, Chögyam. *The Dawn of Tantra*. Berkeley: Shambhala, 1975.

Gyatso, Geshe Kelsang. *Meaningful to Behold*. London: Wisdom, 1980.